BEHIND THE EYES

Edgell Rickword

BEHIND THE EYES
Selected Poems & Translations

CARCANET NEW PRESS

SBN 85635 075 3

First published in 1976
by Carcanet New Press Limited
in association with
Carcanet Press Limited
330-332 Corn Exchange Buildings
Manchester M4 3BG

Printed in Great Britain
by Eyre & Spottiswoode Limited
at Grosvenor Press, Portsmouth

CONTENTS

THE BUTTERFLIES ARE FOR BEATRIX

E. R.

NOTE

The poems in this collection appear in roughly chronological order. They are drawn mainly from the author's three volumes, *Behind the Eyes*, *Invocations to Angels* and *Twittingpan*. The text incorporates his latest revisions and includes some previously unpublished material. In effect the author regards this as a *complete* poems—all that he wishes to preserve.

BEHIND THE EYES

THE SOLDIER ADDRESSES HIS BODY

I shall be mad if you get smashed about,
we've had good times together, you and I;
although you groused a bit when luck was out,
say a girl turned us down, or we went dry.

But there's a world of things we haven't done,
countries not seen, where people do strange things;
eat fish alive, and mimic in the sun
the solemn gestures of their stone-grey kings.

I've heard of forests that are dim at noon
where snakes and creepers wrestle all day long;
where vivid beasts grow pale with the full moon,
gibber and cry, and wail a mad old song;

because at the full moon the Hippogriff
with crinkled ivory snout and agate feet,
with his green eye will glare them cold and stiff
for the coward Wyvern to come down and eat.

Vodka and kvass, and bitter mountain wines
we've never drunk; nor snatched the bursting grapes
to pelt slim girls among Sicilian vines,
who'd flicker through the leaves, faint frolic shapes.

Yes, there's a world of things we've never done,
but it's a sweat to knock them into rhyme,
let's have a drink, and give the cards a run
and leave dull verse to the dull peaceful time.

Colonel Cold strode up the Line
   (tabs of rime and spurs of ice);
stiffened all that met his glare:
   horses, men, and lice.

Visited a forward post,
   left them burning, ear to foot;
fingers stuck to biting steel,
   toes to frozen boot.

Stalked on into No Man's Land,
   turned the wire to fleecy wool,
iron stakes to sugar sticks
   snapping at a pull.

Those who watched with hoary eyes
   saw two figures gleaming there;
Hauptmann Kälte, Colonel Cold,
   gaunt in the grey air.

Stiffly, tinkling spurs they moved,
   glassy-eyed, with glinting heel
stabbing those who lingered there
   torn by screaming steel.

I knew a man, he was my chum,
but he grew darker day by day,
and would not brush the flies away,
nor blanch however fierce the hum
of passing shells; I used to read,
to rouse him, random things from Donne —
like 'Get with child a mandrake-root.'
But you can tell he was far gone,
for he lay gaping, mackerel-eyed,
and stiff and senseless as a post
even when that old poet cried
'I long to talk with some old lover's ghost.'

I tried the Elegies one day,
but he, because he heard me say:
'What needst thou have more covering than a man?'
grinned nastily, so then I knew
the worms had got his brains at last.
There was one thing I still might do
to starve those worms; I racked my head
for wholesome lines and quoted *Maud*.
His grin got worse and I could see
he sneered at passion's purity.
He stank so badly, though we were great chums
I had to leave him; then rats ate his thumbs.

In sodden trenches I have heard men speak,
though numb and wretched, wise and witty things;
and loved them for the stubbornness that clings
longest to laughter when Death's pulleys creak;

and seeing cool nurses move on tireless feet
to do abominable things with grace,
dreamed them dear sisters in that haunted place
where, with child's voices, strong men howl or bleat.

Yet now those men lay stubborn courage by,
riding dull-eyed and silent in the train
to old-man stools; or sell gay-coloured socks
and listen fearfully for Death; so I
love the low-laughing girls, who now again
go daintily, in thin and flowery frocks.

ADVICE TO A GIRL FROM THE WAR

Weep for me half a day,
    then dry your eyes.
Think! is a mess of clay
    worth a girl's sighs?

Sigh three days if you can
    for my waste blood.
Think then, you love a man
    whose face is mud;

whose flesh and hair thrill not
    to any touch.
Dear! best things soonest rot!
    Dream not of such!

DEAD OF NIGHT

It is cold in that seething world
    where only shadows grow.
There dark ferns with misty fronds
    sway to and fro.

And silent birds build nests of cloud
    among the thin grey leaves.
Some beast toiling underground
    mountains upheaves.

Through banks of fog run raving streams,
    the cruel dry water shrills
rushing to black hollow seas
    down shaking hills.

In meadows by the river-side
    where flames the sharp spear-grass,
boys and girls wander naked
    on points of glass.

Flat-breasted girls with spongey eyes,
    their hair is crumbling sand;
their laugh freezes in the air
    as hand in hand,

they drift from ashy bloom to bloom
    with weary shoulders bent,
vaguely, unknowing, seeking
    colour or scent.

Yet they are gay when the night comes
    and by a rotting lake,
from lascivious thigh-bones
    wild music shake.

With my hollow bones' tip-tapping
    mixes their rustling hair;
rattling bones and rustling sand
    make music there.

Then the girls' long, sharp fingers string
    their screaming violins
with my taut nerves, and the night's
    mad joy begins.

And the boys gamble fiercely
    when the heavy night falls,
for my sleepless senses, ears
    tongue and eyeballs.

So an empty body I lie
    until the new bright day
brings colours back, boys and girls
    then slink away.

When the sun brings bright colours back
    birds are noisy again;
green leaves and white flowers tap
    my window-pane.

17

SEA SASH

These are eternal waves that slowly surge
Between the ears, till earthly music fades,
And images from Memory emerge
Into the crystal sunlight of the past.

It is an old wind, and has long been stilled
That moves those waters; and the sun that rose
Above the sea, and with warm radiance filled
The quietness, is a cold grey bubble now.

Only one figure lingers on the sand,
Singing as softly as the falling waves;
With slim white feet the foam encircles, and
Across her breast a broad, green, dripping weed.

BLINDNESS

They were five Princes once, white-horsed and plumed,
cantering through the gorges of the night,
where dark magnolias nodded, star-light foamed
and cataracts crashed down with iron might.

A score of hooves on the hollow sounding floor
drummed in their ears deep music, till they came
panting at sunrise to a purple heath
and halted, silent, wreathed in tossing flame.

They spurred across the heather, and at noon
splashed in the violet pools like tiger-cubs;
but one who scooped red honey from the rocks
saw eyes that watched him in the glistening shrubs.

And in the still noon they heard falling seas
far off, and tightened girths and journeyed on;
those four white-mounted Princes by whose side
a shadowy horseman rode, cave-eyed and wan.

Now in their fragile kingdoms they are sad
ruling the phantoms in dark Memory's caves;
but he is sadder than his brother kings
who stares unceasingly across the waves,

where his white body by the silent pool
glistens like snow within the crystal air
that lovely forms inhabit, though for him
no flowers or trees or maidens burgeon there.

THE TIRED LOVER
(After Théophile Gautier)

Sheila and Pam and you, Olive and Joan,
your laughter wearies me and the old tricks fail.
I love one now who is quiet, and very pale;
her hair is of dark gold and her name Yvonne.

She is fifteen, and lives in a white tower
by the Yellow River. Her father is old
and all day and night counts up his hoarded gold.
He does not see that the peach-tree is in flower.

From a high window she leans out and sings;
the swallows fly to her breast and nestle there;
and in the cool evening she lets down her hair
that draws the great moths to it and burns their wings.

But I sit beneath it and rest from a long war,
being tired of the full sun and too much light.
Her hair brushes my mouth, and in the night
I gaze at her face, that is far away, like a star.

DESIRE

As the white sails of ships across the ocean
the last sounds fade when the sun has declined;
I am alone; there is no motion
rippling the clear waters of the mind.

Only now the madrepores' frail tentacles
sway languidly before they fall asleep;
and waiting in their dark pinnacles
the virgin medusae watch and weep.

Moving darkly amongst the forests of weed
ancient memories drag their crinkled shells
to glades where crimson tree-trunks bleed
thickly, and hushed are the faint sea-bells.

Out of that silent depth loveless arising
Undine sheds on the water her shining hair;
sadly yearns for her soul, devising
a fragrance of music through the wide air.

KEEPSAKE
(After Albert Samain)

Her dress was of tulle, flowered with pale roses
and rose-pale were her lips, and her eyes cold
and blue as the dreaming waters deep forests hold.
The languorous Tyrhennian assuaged her sad hours
with its gentle waves. Very quietly she lay,
crossing her slender feet, and clearly, softly singing
songs that awoke the sorrow of childhood's ending.
On her wrist was the sign of her exile, an iron band
where her name was written, *Stephania*, her white name.
She died in a mist of flowers, watching the sails
that lay on the sea wrapped in autumnal veils.
She died in the fall of the year, towards winter,
and it seemed that a sound of music had faded away.

LOVERS

'Sheila, why do you lid your eyes
    in this shadowy place?
Is there terror where these green leaves throng
    that you hide a flower-pale face?
What gay-plumed bird that rends the air
    puts pain or sorrow in his song
    or screams of horror there?'

'Lover, these trees are withered men,
    horny and dry of touch;
they have waited many hungry springs
    for some hollow soul to clutch;
I fear they wrap me now away
    where neither bird nor maiden sings,
    but silent shadows sway.

That ancient world within those trunks
    and empty dark-roofed boughs,
gapes for another spirit to seize,
    to be its cold prison-house.
Its eyes upon me wake wild fears
    that I may shiver here like these,
    all my young, lovely years.'

'Sweet, these are oak and beech around,
    kindly and honest trees;
they have no wolfish eyes that gleam
    like still and dreadful seas.'
'Love, kiss away these thoughts that throng,
    you are so brave you cannot dream,
    so blind you are, so strong.'

DALLIANCE

How can you gather up your hair
    with languid hands before your glass,
knowing, with deep-set instinct, love
    flowers as brief time as summer grass?
How bind your hair and braid your hair
    as though love's days would never pass?

Will you set candles like tall ghosts
    beside your mirror when the moan
of darkening winds around the house
    wakes the old misery in old stone;
and slowly weave strange loveliness
    for silent flame and glass alone?

Beyond your windows even now
    sweep the last petals, deathly white;
into cold lands behind the hills
    droops the red blossom of the light;
yet you caress only your hair
    and lie with shadows through the night.

The thin wraiths tremble, like a breath
    the Forest and the Blossoms fade
as the dark cloud of moth-winged years
    folds all her hair about with shade,
and the deep mirror's pools are void
    of Flowers of Flame, or Hair, or Maid.

A CHILD

There is no tree like Janet;
  though swaying in the breeze
no tree has boughs like her arms
  when she raises them to wave.
Her slender hands are paler
  than candle-flames at sunrise;
no fluttering moths at summer dusk
  so swift as her grey eyes.

There will be trees as graceful
  and gentle, grey-eyed flowers;
in shady woods and hedgerows
  swift dove-like moths will hover,
when with sad voices hurrying winds
  usher her spirit to far seas.

YEGOR

' "What shall I write?" said Yegor.'—Tchehov

'What shall I write?' said Yegor.
   'Of the bright-plumed bird that sings
hovering on the fringes of the forest
   where leafy dreams are grown,
and thoughts go with silent flutterings
   like moths by a dark wind blown?'

'O, write of those quiet women
   beautiful, slim, and pale,
whose bodies glimmer under cool green waters,
   whose hands like lilies float
tangled in the heavy purple veil
   of tresses on breast and throat.

'Or write of swans and princes
   carved in white marble clouds;
of the flowers that wither upon distant mountains,
   grey-pencilled in the brain.
Of fiercely hurrying, night-born crowds
   by the first swift sun-ray slain.'

'Nay, I will sing,' said Yegor,
   'of stranger things than these.
Of a girl I met in the fresh of morning,
   a laughing, slender flame.
Of the slow stream's song and the chant of bees,
   in a land without a name.'

WINTER PROPHECIES

Cities with tall and graceful spires I know
mirrored in pools and rivers silver bright,
that wither if the softest wind should blow,
and by a stone are blotted out of sight.

Frailer they are than curving leaves of snow
that flutter down from the dark trees of night
slowly, and then unutterably slow,
and ceasing, as most quietly comes the light.

Water is carved like fern and stone takes on
the flush of life now flesh lies quiet as stone;
whilst sinister and clownish, bright and wan
with solemn affectations the old moon
spins dooms and weirds and meltings of the bone
and universal silence to be soon.

COMPLAINT OF A TADPOLE
CONFINED IN A JAM-JAR

What reveries of far-off days
these withered plaques of duck-weed raise!

The creeping wretches, the crowded Pond,
a Death-in-Life, no Culture, no Beyond;

Light and No-light in dull routine;
Thought and No-thought two shades of green;

the fair ideals all creatures need
smothered beneath th'inferior weed,

since highest Aspirations stop,
for tadpoles, at the water-top!

O Faery Metamorphosis,
for Being to become What-Is!

Here ceaseless radiance fills my Sphere,
The Lamp my Moon, all night, bright, near.

And clustering on the crystal wall
great Strawberries, iconistical.

No strife to propagate the Kind,
but leisure to improve the Mind!

Yet curious sensations range
about the tail, and hint at change.

The weed with flowers stars the sky
and monstrous Forms sweep dimly by.

Tail fades! the vestiges of gills
swell with rare Aether from the hills

which Time reared up in rocky crests
where flaming Fowl involve their nests;

whilst in the valleys pipers play
Over the hills and far away.

INTIMACY

Since I have seen you do those intimate things
that other men but dream of; lull asleep
the sinister dark forest of your hair
and tie the bows that stir on your calm breast
faintly as leaves that shudder in their sleep;
since I have seen your stocking swallow up,
a swift black wind, the flame of your pale foot,
and feigned your slender legs so meshed in silk
twin mermaid sisters drowned in their sleek hair—
I have not troubled overmuch with food,
and wine has seemed like water from a well;
pavements are built of fire, grass of thin flames;
all other girls grow dull as painted flowers
or flutter harmlessly like coloured flies
whose wings are tangled in the net of leaves
spread by thin boughs that grow behind your eyes.

OUTLINE OF HISTORY

I.
A little shaggy creature, sullen-eyed,
from the dark entrance to his cave stared out,
and watched the Moon in frozen silence glide
above the sweating forests, and the rout
of screaming beasts who bred, or slew, or died.

He felt that distant spirit sway the seas,
and strangely sway his sense with passionate
forebodings of eternal ecstasies;
and snarling at his tousled dirty mate,
stamped from his den to prowl among the trees.

II.
The woods were thronging with white forms of maidens
through sunny glades and shady alleys dancing;
and sleek-haired frisky goatmen, raucous-laughtered,
from girl to girl with woodland gifts went prancing;
light-foot he roamed through countries many-watered,
full of clear streams with shining silver sand-beds
and lushy pastures where great beasts were feeding,
with smooth black pelts and gleaming ivoried foreheads.
He saw the blue stone of the night sky bleeding
bright gouts of gold, and swan-white creatures winging
over high mountains where he could not follow.
They saddened him with faint unearthly singing
till all his new-found world grew thin and hollow
as a glass bubble; and like moonlight shadows
the laughing dancers swept across the meadows.

III.
Flowers burgeoned out of stone, and mountains thrust
from clouds of music their white jagged peaks;
women with wilder eyes and paler cheeks
than tears give women, grew from coloured dust;
and crystal cities blossomed out of words,
with green seas foaming round their marble walls,
with rich fern-bordered lawns and snow-flecked falls,
and Bakst Princesses gay as parakeets.

30

IV.
Rayless and swollen hangs the dying sun;
the leaden sky is empty, and alone
the earth swings slowly round from dusk to dusk.
Under the heavy air the mountains rust;
the stagnant rivers rot in sombre meadows;
the flowers are harsh and grey, the trees are shadows.
The lank-haired cattle shiver on the hills,
and bellow as the long night slowly falls
that freezes the live marrow in their groins
and strews the earth with silent mottled stones.
The twinkling fires break out among the cliffs,
marking the entrance to the deepest clefts,
and vague forms clumsily reel to and fro
bearing enormous trunks, and stumble through
the smoke and flame to build up shadowy mounds
out of the forests that have crumbled down.
The tousled girls, coarse limbed, with clawy hands,
chatter together, squatting on their hams,
and dully wait for darkness, and the cold
that creeps, a thin foam-line of glittering fire,
down from the peaks, and stiffens beast and flower
with a white covering of shining wool.
Out of the dusk it glistens, and those shapes
creep from their fires and stagger through the earth,
down into darkness where some warmth still hangs,
down through the deepest tunnel, till their hands
tear impotently at the solid rock.
Outside the flames are frozen, and the ash
lies grey and ghastly that was once a tree . . .

REGRET FOR THE PASSING OF
THE ENTIRE SCHEME OF THINGS

Now in the midst of Summer stay the mind
whilst flowers hold their stony faces up
and fishes peer through crystal vacancies.

For even in these drowsy hours of ease
Winter's white-armoured horsemen on the hills
take from the virgin Frost their stirrup-cup . . .

Whilst now in dusky corners lovers kiss
and goodmen smoke their pipes by tiny gates—
these oldest griefs of Summer seem less sad

than drone of mowers on suburban lawns
and girls' thin laughter, to the ears that hear
the soft rain falling of the failing stars.

GRAVE JOYS

When our spent bodies moulder underground,
shut off from these bright waters and clear skies;
when we hear nothing but the sullen sound
of dead flesh dropping slowly from the bone
and muffled fall of tongue and ears and eyes;
perhaps, as each disintegrates alone,
frail broken vials once brimmed with curious sense,
our souls will pitch old Grossness from his throne
and on the beat of unsubstantial wings
soar to new ecstasies still more intense.
There the thin voices of black horny things
shall thrill me as girls' laughter thrills me here,
and the cold drops a passing storm-cloud flings
be my strong wine, and crawling roots and clods
my trees and hills, and slugs swift fallow deer.
There I shall dote upon a sexless flower
by ghost-love planted in my dripping brain
and suck from those cold petals subtler power
than drained from your warm flesh and clinging curls,
most lovely, vile, adorable of girls.
But in your tomb th'immortal She will reign,
drawing fresh lovers out of tangled sods;
so your lithe spirit may till Doomsday squirm
under the weird embraces of the worm.

C

Out of dark rooms they loom like vessels moored
by lapping wharves, that wait the evening tide
with white sails furled. But this immortal Stream
is ever at the flood, and all winds serve
mortality's strange voyages on the depths
or shoreward shallows of Sleep's unknown seas.
For there's no respite from the pains of birth
though calmest midnight toll on silent fields;
and in the morning's pale unpassioned light
men scan the faces that last night were strange
and turn to dream unsatisfied. The old
may seek their feeble visions out at noon,
for Sleep stays not for darkness, nor will Night,
with every star put out, bring peace to one
desiring past companionship in vain.
But when the Body struggles not, and thoughts
that thronged the common highways of the brain
on automatic errands, are released,
the Creature goes wing-footed through the world
of visible and invisible substance.
It can fly
swifter than light, pursuing vain regrets
into the past, and hover in the serene
of Cressida before her treacherous days;
desire burns not, for that dark teasing of the brain,
the thin-lipped Thais, is unborn, and lies
patiently in the loins of some rough man
who labours in tranquillity unshamed;
and beating through the sombre leafless boughs
of giant forests oozing by warm seas
probe beneath clumsy monsters' iron hides
for the brute peace humanity denies;
but in the dim retreat behind their eyes
lurk unsuspected torments; questionings
of worse and better rack their pitiful minds
and they know not contentment. Even dust
that struggles in the sticky depths of Space
still thrusts towards its centre, and new suns,
by slow gestation built in darkness, gleam
and waken fresh illusions into life.

The Creature flags; wings set against the Stream
weaken, and too-far-off simplicity
foils the intense endeavour. The strong tide
unhurrying sweeps it forward until high
and glittering cities by Earth's shackled seas
rise, with their delicate spires and jutting eaves
fretting a fern-leaf pattern in clear skies.
But these too dimly wither in the strange mists
of backward Time, and are not found again
even by yearning eyes. Yet rarer forms
flourish on mountain tops and on Pole snows,
not made by hands and garmenting no soul;
deserted courts, aisles barren, hostels built
for guests invisible or fled; white homes
now sullied, sagging like a past year's nests,
now cold, now empty . . . The winged wanderer foiled
finds fragile shelter from the unending quest
in homely linen by the banks of life,
awaiting winds of either Death or Dream
to waft him to new continents unguessed
and unimaginable fêtes — alone,
or lonelier companioned, on frail barques
set in the cities' honeycomb, that loom
out of dark rooms like vessels with sails furled,
by dusky wharves waiting the evening tide.

OBSESSION

That swift bird Passion flown, such silence falls
on the bed-chamber that my spirit goes
a lonely pilgrimage to seek repose
through the dark world enclosed within the walls;
but there the savour of the hidden Rose
that He has mangled, her warm flesh recalls;
and from far mountain-snows slow waterfalls
make such soft music as her breathing does.

There is no peace, my Spirit, though we fled
into the furthest forests the flowers there
would seem symbolical and speak of her;
yet it is terrible to feel her stir,
and the continual sense of her that clings
about the mouth entangled in her hair;
and that swift Bird returning to our bed
with sombre throbbing of remorseless wings.

COSMOGONY

Cosmic Leviathan, that monstrous fish,
stirred in his ancient sleep, begins to dream;
and out of nothingness dishevelled suns
crawl, with live planets tangled in their hair.

And through the valleys of those phantom worlds
some pursue shadows painfully, and grasp
the husks they see, and name one Rose, and one
Willow, that leans and whispers over pools.

They speak of mountains reared and crashing seas
and forests that seem older than the hills;
or meet a maiden-shade and plan with her
sojourn and rapture in Eternity.

Slowly the sunrise breaks beyond those hills,
by waveless seas; and in the golden light,
heavy with his long sleep Leviathan
splashes, and half recalls a waking dream.

COMPLAINT AFTER PSYCHO-ANALYSIS

Now my days are all undone,
spirit sunken, girls forgone,
I shall weave in other mesh
than fading bone and flesh.

Into cold deserted mind
drag the relics of the blind;
and raise from wives none other sees
substantial families.

Hunt through woods of maidenhair
tangled in the shining air
the forms of ecstasies achieved —
not then believed.

O Unicorns and jewelled Birds
and trampling dappled moonlight Herds,
in icy glades now slain
with arrows bright as pain!

Leap, Moon, from the berg's pale womb!
Frail Bride, out of Earth's tomb!
The stars are ashen cold
beneath their gold.

INVOCATIONS TO ANGELS

TERMINOLOGY

Trees have been named and brutes with shining skins,
and in pure darkness many a planet spins
no living eyes have seen, yet men say *Three*
Orion's gathering in his massy hair.
New stars will burn when all our lights are gone.
Our world runs slower and our sun grows wan
lighting pale crowds that tease the city's edge
like nerveless rags caught on a gusty hedge,
until from Time's cold mirror or deep mind
firm syllables beckon them to shapes designed.
But Ecstasy that lofty unicorn
starts at the summons of no common horn,
lingering ghostly in mysterious moods
a milk-white angel hid in flowering woods;
and if no signal from its fastness comes
we still lie shrouded in sepulchral homes;
speech being precious when the word we use
leaps to an end beyond our power to choose,
when it bids *leopard* from the accustomed haze
break and like fire glide down his leafy ways;
or drawing softly back the sea's rich veil
reveals domestic the grave monarch *whale*;
the god-filled Adam designating brutes,
each to its pied or sombre attributes.

These may be emanations out of Sense,
dissolving shapes, vortices in the dense
and universal stillness where such birds
lie folded as have never winged from words,
and new-framed qualities not more pure and free
from concrete alloy than our He and She:
departments not yet opened, promised lands,
the late reward of eager eyes and hands.
These, if not permanent nor perhaps the best,
are tangible treasure and kind only breast
for the earth-haunted mind that moves obscure
among symbolical forests seeking pure
immutable forms in which to crystallise
the word-skinned phantoms that delight our eyes,
till through its paroxysms, pangs, deceits

of sense and reason or slow brutish heats,
the tried, familiar trees and fair-named flowers
shut in the four-fold stuff of space and hours,
thought's patient elements; and women grown
too docile under habits not their own;
bright incarnations damned to trivial calls
like shirted angels nailed to bedroom walls;
and all tense lives subdued to what they seem,
shed their coarse husks and naked in Time's stream
stand up unsullied out of the sun's beam.

The world's lit up and all made festival:
it is a spacious, quaintly furnished hall.
Flung from each mountain-wall festoons
of odorous trees enwreathe the air,
where Mind advances mazed with moons
only down pathways the blood wore;
and all its antique ceremonial
must be endured till nerves like ushers cry,
'Retire, retire! The Queen shines here no more.'
Then the flowered hangings are laid by,
the fountains' silver plumes thrown down,
but, as spectators linger where
royalty has passed, when youth is flown
the senses weary on their mountain-rims
observe Death's servants empty earth's vast hall
and last, put out the tapers of bright limbs.

TRANSPARENCY

The mind is a shaft of ice
light frets with a curious device
of bent and branching streets
that are forest to many feet.

From his lair the leopard roams
down the rows of ordered homes
and the ancient serpent winds
softly, through the lowered blind.

Bright as fish, their glittering robes
haunt a melancholy globe;
though bedded deep as ambered bees
their deathless fury stalks at ease.

In this rock each moves fire-laden
using shapes of moon and maiden:
as Wonder, burning all to tears,
when Joy, the fragrant leopard, nears.

THE CASCADE

Lovers may find similitudes
to the sweet babbling girlish noise,
in the unhuman crystal voice
that calls from mountain solitudes;

as that's but movement overlaid
with water, a faint shining thought,
spirit is to music wrought
in the swift passion of a maid.

It is her body sings so clear,
chanting in the woods of night;
on Earth's dark precipice a white
Prometheus, bound like water here;

the eager Joys toward their task
from dusky veins beat up in flocks,
but still her curious patience mocks
the consummation lovers ask.

Lying on ferns she seems to wear
(the silver tissue of the skin
radiant from the fire within)
light as her weed and shade for hair;

rapt in communion so intense
the nicer senses fail and she,
sweet Phoenix, burns on Pain's rich tree
in praise and prayer and frankincense.

The iron beaks that seek her flesh
vex more her lovers' anxious minds,
in whose dim glades each hunter finds
his own torn spirit in his mesh.

STRANGE PARTY
'Votre âme est un paysage choisi...'—Paul Verlaine

On that lawn's most secret shade
joy-masked, your thoughts droop in their dance,
as though your spirit, overweighed,
tired of the saxophone's pert nonchalance;

their arms gay gestures still intend,
gently their voices lapse, and cold
the cascades of the moon descend
on shadowy dancers with false cheeks of gold.

Discreetly mocking in the gloom
those masqueraders bow and twirl,
feigning to exorcise the doom
that seals the fountains of your heart, queer girl.

DREAM AND POETRY
'Helen was not up, was she?'—Pandarus

Helen sleeps still, her stockings lie,
black branches, on a snowy sky.
From Troy's hearths rise faint trees of smoke
out of the needs of common folk.

But now her mind is a green glade
where wanders a quite harmless maid
nursing the still fire in her blood
in mere wanton lassitude.

Through grape-dark veins wind-softly ran
death's unobtrusive caravan;
from breast to breast and lips to feet
as though along a falling street.

The pool her image falls upon
holds fast as ice that captive swan;
lilies in mirrored branches caught
are joys entangled in her thought.

Mind mirrors mind, whose limpid grace
draws down the perfect, thoughtless face
to lift up from its silver slime
clear brows that pierce the glass of Time.

And when she leaves her secret ways
gowned in a slender silken phrase,
doomed Body's sentinels appear
as trees or stars fast-frozen here.

ANNIHILATION

My cat and dog dream not as I. This room
is their smooth field, hazardous but not strange;
tall flowers stand there biting at the touch
and half my wisdom hangs upon that bloom;

for when those candles fade we are shut up;
sight gone, no sense responds to summons much;
but darkness is a world the beast may range
and miss no stone the orphic sun built up.

Light gone, my books are dumb for me or cat,
taste wanes, smell fails, the fingers hardly wake;
my dog cocks ears at a familiar foot
and greets my love before my brain thinks that.

Dark holds Earth rigid, in whose bowl of hills
silence flows down, a soft reflecting lake
filled with this velvet, gold-flecked scene whose root
my Thought leans over, sighing as it kills.

FAREWELL TO FANCY
The Suburb of Adolescence Revisited

The evening villas smoke and doze
like men from daytime tasks released.
Round each small yard the air is creased
where a thin boundary paling goes.

Like sick men's thoughts the narrow strips
of garden push forth small strange flowers
sown in long-since vague hours
on curious or on shy girl's lips.

The nubile daughters now escape
to any waste or open plot
where flowers or sweethearts may be got
for divination or feigned rape.

On building sites by tall stark poles
sweetly their maiden languor droops.
O dandelions and rusty hoops
and low foundations in their souls!

This is the rock on which we build,
poets or pierrots, our True Church;
the Founder blessing our long search
a boy with amorous mischief filled.

Let us abjure the stately creeds,
love's plangent groves and choristers,
with all that Eloquence confers
upon our elemental needs.

We will go with them by the tram
beyond the city's lamps, and sit,
with such emotions as befit
those born between the *Plough* and *Ram*.

And afterwards the gramophone
in dusky parlours shall delude
our mutual insolicitude
with sentiments that mask our own.

48

BEYOND GOOD AND EVIL

As mountain-pools hold images
of starry clusters and earth's trees
when storm has ceased its ravages,
where birds brood in celestial ease:

when passion passes, in her eyes
the earthly forests of delight
spread their dark leaves against the skies
filled with a snowy bloom of light.

Her thoughts haunt that duplicity
and perch alike on tree and star,
in calm, white-winged simplicity,
innocent as angels' are.

Since, in those blissful powers at least,
thought and act are identified,
it is a part-angelic beast
sleepily smiling at my side.

SIR ORANG HAUT-TON AT VESPERS

'Oh World be nobler for her sake!'—H. Trench

Consider that from topmost peaks
of Time now booms the pale baboon
his solemn rhetoric that breaks
the glacial stillness of the moon.

In glittering skies Desire extends,
past her to whom mere hunger led,
too exquisite for common ends,
a Maid who rules Nature's cold bed.

Earth's quiet forests are of stone
by long rains worn arboreal shapes,
where his grave gestures' shadow thrown
repeats the need of vanished apes.

The slow procession of dead suns
bemuses his rebellious brain,
ogling the apt Machine that runs
with gathered skirt through age-grey rain.

The legs are marble-smooth in hose
and neatly-pointed crocodile
cases not-now-prehensile toes,
but still the simian limbs beguile;

as tram-lines on Bank Holidays
lure to that worn familiar sod
where the Ancestral Tripper plays
in pungent groves the pagan god.

RACE DAY

It is Desire creates our world,
with its great tapers the submissive suns
lighting dark veins where
the virgin spirit her few furlongs runs,
in a race through silence hurled
to the absolute winning-post;
and if these limbs prove too rare
all Heirlooms and Estate are lost.

Slyly judicious, Thought spread his crow-wings,
she had not gone too far and could not climb
out of the bleached and scorching track
the blood scored in the tender grass of time;
so to her small, white flank closer he clings
till her poor bosom labours with her breath,
seeing he waved the sullen black
flag of the judge Death.

Unnatural consummation must take place
in the sophisticated glade,
where she goes in all cold and white
who yet comes out a maid.
Leda beneath the fragrant swan's embrace
conceived divinely, but here netted skies
let fall no bolt nor balm of light
on destined mortal thighs.

Now man's great day is almost done,
the colonels and the touts depart;
still lingers, tiny on the Down,
a huckster by his rifled cart.
The crammed last bus, last Hope, is gone,
and we, benighted, squeamish girls,
coldly regard how, darkly blown,
the crowd's foul pleasure-litter whirls.

BIRTHDAY RUMINATIONS

Now I can see the creeping edge of life,
threaten the cliff where my flesh-image waits;
the semaphore of blanched appealing paws,
dead-leaf skeletons in once-read books,
impotently beckons from the beach.

That sad sea-lumber, barnacled delight,
frets but retards not, founders in, the tide
rattling the relics of our royal state,
lorn Lackland's treasure, drowned Mnemosyne,
mashed in scurf and grit to dumb fish-fodder.

Shall we go down if we can find the steps,
inspect the chaos of dismembered sense,
inquire what beam enticed from native space,
dazzled and dashed against ironic glass,
that wild sea-scourer, the bold gull we knew?

If tears must be associate with despair,
touch follow sight, then both report decay
unless identity can be disproved,
weeping judged wanton, foreign to the loss;
a free creation in a mind at peace.

The crepitation of the restless grains
and the soft integration of fresh worlds
and the vermiculation of the flesh,
is the procession of the pastoral soul;
a piscine epic, mammal tragedy.

NECROPOLIS

'I love you . . . Love you . . . ' murmurs she.
Like the inscription on a tomb
the words bite into me,
buried in the sullen gloom
of Earth's November Sunday-afternoon.

Decayed fertility now wraps me close
in darkness of no-more-desire,
in dank and fusty sheets of fallen rose
rust-edged at touch of fire
expired and glinting coldly as a moon.

Persistent as a pain Joy's humble folk,
eternal pilgrims to the grave,
thread these yew-shaded alleys and invoke
with the poor flowers they have
from careless mind the likeness of its Spring.

The essence ravished from the pudic rose
oozes from Memory's fallen flask,
too-faint cosmetic to impose
on Love's discarded mask,
once bloomed with powder from the night-moth's wing.

Shut in this little hired room
unrestful longings beat in vain
the leaden boundaries of doom;
like an old king whose reign
fades in the peace prodigious wars have made.

For, as our tumbling head-stones shout,
'Consumed in their desires' own noon
thus rapt in space, so crumbles out
passion of Earth and Moon.'
The radiance her's, though just his stock-in-trade.

Dearest, when I smooth your hair
I think neglected fish leap there,
in that Red Sea condemned to hide
till end of Time their scaly pride.

Alas, dumb Flea, we may not hear
the passionate song that once rang clear
when, fallen Philomel, the gale
to the awed woods re-told your tale!

A noble sisterhood of fowl,
white Girl, Fish, Flea and snowy Owl;
Legs, Fins, Wings, Claws, O Instruments!
Relics of cruel banishments.

There is a silence in the mind of each
the fading tramp of Progress does not reach,
where they in solemn rites exult,
the arcane communion of their cult.

Hail and Farewell! Our ways diverge.
Some worthier lyre must lead the dirge,
as the rich ore of your desires
refines to myth round our camp-fires.

Angels! bequeath your tongues of flame
to those who need them more than you;
in Paradise you know no shame
and love blooms not without that dew.

In these grey-leaved suburban groves
we melancholy couples lie,
whom some uncouth persuasion moves
in one another's arms to die.

Our better nature then proceeds
to sublimation of its dross,
and flings a bridge of painted needs
to mansions ransomed by the Cross.

Shall we tread proudly, O my love,
this Jacob's Ladder of escape?
I know you gentler than the dove
whose timid eyes invite the rape;

yet not, I think, so small of mind
as to claim plumage of the Bird
whose dazzling beauty strikes us blind,
though all abstracted from a word.

The swans in flight through winter dusk
seem to man fast in nature's vice,
emblems of power as pure as musk
and first to pride his thoughts entice.

Yet in our earth-bound partnership
such rarely lovely moments rise,
why need Omnipotence equip
perpetual brothels in the skies?*

Let eyes reflect like forest lakes
all beasts to ancient comfort led,
till joy to innocence awakes,
as children hug in some cold bed.

* '. . . in Heaven there is neither marrying nor giving in marriage.'

The sun that lightened the first Easter Day
traced in the arc of his familiar way
the choreography of Resurrection,
which works on our world now, the true reflection
whereby the sun-foot dancer draws the dead
out of the sepulchre of formless dread;
and as the sun still seems to our slow wit
to attend on us when we derive from it
all vital qualities, these verses show
no revelation you did not bestow.

   I had been long immured in that dark tomb
which to my new state was a kind of womb,
for like a child my spirit wrenched and cried
to leave that warm death for the harsh joy outside;
and I had lain there since desire first fled,
sick of my narrow intellectual bed.
Weak as a girl deserted when she loves,
my fancy roamed its dim and hopeless groves
and climbed in turn the five thin towers of sense
out of those dank, autumnal airs of absence
by the whole being realised as pain,
forgotten only to be proved again.
All the horizons of the senses burned
with constellations on old charts discerned;
Thought drooped and wept beneath their ancient fire,
gazing on lands empty of her desire.

   Dawn is a miracle each night debates,
which faith may prophesy but luck dictates.
How long can Earth, our old and heavy dame,
keep at her tumbling trick and not fall lame?
Yet every morning like a girl she lands,
sweeps the hair from her eyes with windy hands,
then smiling at her men on hill and plain
dries off the dew and turns to toil again.

   This daily somersault is not so strange
as the vast orbit the emotions range,
since in the opening of a door they fly

from farthest gloom into a dawn-lit sky,
as errant comets rush from outer space
to fecund ruin on their sun's bright face.

    Not like Eurydice on the verge of light
flung back to Hades and that uncouth twilight —
not as a woman promising a boon
bait me with dawn and cheat me of the noon,
fair Sun, but travel all your broad ellipse,
drawing the planets like a fleet of ships,
till you lean westward and they flash to Earth,
in fiery codes, news of your second birth.

    World-bound as in a glass my spirit runs,
dancing on rippled pools like mimic suns
in fragile ballets with the trees and stars
the old grave histories of immortal scars,
the yet-not-pitiful sorrows, being so deep
it is not eyes but longing minds that weep.

    Reflections perish when the sun has set,
leaving no interval to voice regret.
This threnody of silence will say more
than all the mournful poems made before;
whoever lives to mourn proves by his verse
desire impure, being less than universe.
So my mortality with yours must flow,
not to lie stranded when that tide runs low;
our callow light sink to the quiet breast
where the imperial suns like fledglings nest
and the long-wandering cuckoo-fires find rest.

ABSENCES

I.

Time's landscape is all bare,
    deserted stone,
once in darkening air
    desire is gone.

Effort can bring no bloom
    to hang there, nor water
to lighten the gloom
    in solitude, of matter.

Thought stirs not the rock
    of mind, that mountain;
but a girl's empty frock,
    a moonlit fountain

whence the chill fragrance falls
    of love in past hours,
plashing the stony walls
    sets moss there and flowers.

II.

In the solitude of soul
only echo answered me,
till my longing in despair
grew incorporate with air.

Then, O Shadow, no control
bounded our twin unity,
and the land grew soft as moss
gentle thoughts barefoot might cross.

Guileless figures came and went,
creating it a place of calm.
Neither Self nor shadow move
in the atmosphere of love.

One above the other bent
like willows in a pool of balm;
air so luminous that Shade
one with Self true Circle made.

Now is Joy's own image spilled
and the landscape in eclipse
has the crumpled emptiness
of a just discarded dress.

All the scene that Self had willed
a mirror, so to ruin slips.
No lake, no glass will now return
the form with which, lonely, I burn.

III.
Now that you lie in lonely pain,
O Moon in no flower-clouded bed,
what shall evoke our joy again?
Rain Tears, harsh Tears where Fancy fled!

Under their sharp, caressing stroke
the foliage of our love revives,
though your face pale when anguish broke
alone on night's dead sea survives.

LUXURY

The long, sleek cars rasp softly on the kerb
and chattering women rise from cushioned nests,
flamingo-tall, whose coral legs disturb
the mirror-surface where creation rests.

Aconite, Opium, Mandragora, Girl!
Essential phials exquisite array!
Poisons whose frail, consumptive fervours whirl
the stony city to a fierce decay.

The churches' sun-dried clay crumbles at last,
the Courts of Justice wither like a stink
and honourable statues melt as fast
as greasy garbage down a kitchen-sink.

Commercial palaces, hotels de luxe
and Banks in white, immutable ravines,
life's skeleton unfleshed by cynic rooks,
remain to warn the traveller what it means.

The shady universe, once haunt of play,
in leafless winter bares its ways of stone;
the paths we shared, the mounds on which we lay
were ruled by Time and lifted by old bone.

Time has no pity for this world of graves
nor for its dead decked out in feathery shrouds.
The ghoul must perish with the flesh he craves
when stars' hoarse bells of doom toll in the clouds.

CIRCUS

The city empties of its dusky streams,
minnows of industry and honest pride,
and in the arc-lamps' purple glamour seems
a sparkling lake where rainbow pleasures glide.

There the young whores enticing to the sense
seem not to see their next-year image pass,
the dropsied trull that strips their poor pretence
like a reflection in a dirty glass.

In sordid Games the martyrs of desire;
Shame's proselytes, exempt from banal fears;
they mock Solicitude heaping up their fire
whilst Pity gluttonously licks her tears.

In brief lucidity on the ledge of night
we clutch respite from day's abysmal vow,
but those red, wound-lipped mouths abuse more light
and, witchcraft flowers, must be curse-gathered now.

Dawn's candid sky is thick with flying robes
as if, curt visitor to a pauper's bed,
questioning gangrened hopes with spartan probes,
an antique Virtue had been here and fled!

The morning's pleasant bustle frees them not
from stupor's dreary, cellular repose,
while the unseen sun prepares the next night's plot
with worn devices timid lusts propose.

Between low walls whose faded paper mocks
with painted blossoms bridals of the air
when lovers lay at will among their flocks,
a common scene stripped love's fresh branches bare.

Out of the ruin an old candour cried
like a man speaking to a faithless friend:
'Now hangman pleasure's triple knot is tied
and we must share one halter till the end.

'So priest and victim in the antique glade
felt the peculiar bond compress their heart,
gazing in awed communion on the blade
that binds the creatures it would seem to part.

'My love is like an anchorite who frets
in ecstasy upon his couch of stone,
so little in me moves toward hate or whets
the steel of vengeance on a wrong once done.

'The modern crowd that laps up tears for blood
takes in such errors with its Sunday milk,
but there's a dualism in my mood
and rapture tears my anguish like fine silk.

'My soul's a trampled duelling-ground where Sade,
the gallant marquis, fences for his life
against the invulnerable retrograde
Masoch, his shade, more constant than a wife.'

The woman sobbing on the bed apart
restored her visage for the endless play,
but the men, lacking the resource of art,
took up their hats like burdens for the day.

She is a solitude in which arise
no wings to break the tranquil eyes' repose,
an arctic stillness where the traveller lies
dazed with such silence in such perfect snows.

The plains of innocence and childish pride
yield not like ice to tracks of prowling fears,
though my hot-muzzled passion gnaws her side
to turn that ecstasy to delirious tears.

I only live to watch her winter thaw
and calm perfection suffer human doom,
the humble instrument of natural law
who signed these warrants in Time's tropic womb.

Into that fastness pours the loosening wind,
Fancy, the pollen-bearer, ravaging flowers;
but musical with meanings for the mind
grown wise in virgin and untutored hours.

The budding woods rise up in tinted mists,
the leaping streams sparkle like silver lambs,
and in the jewel sky the cloud-root twists,
that soon clear heaven with massy foliage crams.

The herald birds trumpet the end's approach
and the last crystal melts into the sun.
Good people, let my fate be your reproach,
swamped in the ruin I'd not willed begun.

POET TO PUNK

'Aux hommes déclassés peut-être l'avenir appartient-il'
                                   Charles Baudelaire

I. *The Deluge*

Now that the light's grim daily duty's done
silence and shadow mitigate despair,
only the split-man frets to sit alone
convoking visions to a squalid lair.

Now London lies a garden to our eyes
where night's tall heliotropes still coldly blaze,
her poets rack the Roget of the skies
but a bilked ponce chokes up the perfect phrase.

Among these streets my vagrant fancy roams
for scraps of sympathy, love's well-scraped bones,
but the beds creaking in a million homes
with nature's vast excuses proffer stones.

My body leans, that beggar emaciate,
starved of all solace, at the open sash.
Night-long I burn in candour's hollow grate
till housemaid morning sifts my wasted ash.

I have a wealth of words to thrill your ear,
(my soul drips honey though my pen seem tart).
If I had your number, my postulated dear,
this is the conversation I would start.

'I am the Noah of the final Flood
and preach precaution to an ironic Park.
To you, related by closer ties than blood,
I offer the sole ticket for my ark.

'When the last spires tilt to the rising waves
and what was city seems a foundered fleet,
we shall lean out and peer in sumptuous caves
once interdict to our laborious feet;

'whilst in mid-depth a medalled dolphin rolls,
the unctuous brutal warden of those rich gates,
whose rot-racked eyes focus the tattered drolls,
dis-ranked, but rankly female, that sprawl the slates;

'whilst putrefaction dyes the taunting flesh
whose the world was, though not, it seems, for keeps —
cover the chasm with mourning's ashen mesh
before my incorrigible mercy weeps.

'Then out oars, and avoid the miasmal bed
to which our low first parents still aspire;
Adam in me, in you Eve grieves to tread
a world not moulded to the heart's desire.

'We'll spend eternity in an open boat,
like a fresh sort of Sunday up the Thames,
cleansed of the journals' sickly antidote
in a purgation their stout world contemns.

'I have no fortune to lay out on stores;
no animal but you joins me for love
or keep. How query the presumptive shores
unless hope hatches faith's poor innocent dove?

'No wing may pierce that calm, last, vast, daft scene;
no beak pillage unimaginable banks.
Now gods abandon this effete machine
the future functions through our rejected flanks.

'Meet me *Tomorrow* then, the edge of Time,
that jetty in the ungovernable waste
where you and I, gaunt rats, cautious in crime,
embark our longings and transpose distaste.'

II. *The Epitaph*

Stray poem whose ill-handled leaves I thumb,
what language gave you birth? What rhymes unheard
echo in vacancies of our spoken word?
Held on the beat of Time's barbaric drum,

our bodies poised wait their obedient fall,
most pliant partners in the jazz of death,
content to break, and claim not one more breath
together, when my rival treads the hall;

of infidelity most docile slaves,
twin paragons of a perfidious age,
paladins of defeat, past hope or salvage;
the horn unanswered, th'unguarded banner waves.

The flash successes of the screen and press,
honour's new legions, counter our disdain;
and too distraught to lyricise our pain
we merge distinctions in a bland caress.

Vaguely uneasy at our degraded lot,
I envy your craft's austere, hieratic rites;
in eyes, lips, hands your simpler nature writes
the humble epitaph to our common rot.

This I transcribe from off our fever's tomb,
seeking in formula what you act by heart;
no meretricious metrics for life's art
nor a perfunctory rhetoric of doom:

'They reaped the tedious harvest of the eye,
not contumacious to the laws of dust;
content to suffer and avoid the just,
numb with the gradual ruin of the sky.'

RIMBAUD IN AFRICA
In the character of the Damned Conjurer

Through my small town I roamed, a taunting ghost
out of a world like rock and wind to yours,
and counted friends and honour nothing lost
to feed the inner pride that burned my hours.

Faustus, whom your academy once crowned,
spent midnight oil on ill-spelt smutty books;
your approbation's dirty insult drowned
in comradeship with idiots and crooks.

Beauty is epicene, whipped slave to show,
yet Helen swan-like glided to his bed,
whom he put scornfully away as though
he sought no pleasure in the life he led.

Such hot disdain scorched desert solitude
around him, where he practised magic art;
from elemental soul sublimed a crude
companion who would share no human heart;

all the devotion of his spirit yearned
on this frail vessel and refined its clay
till with slow eyes it answered him and turned
his pride to wings and went its lonely way.

Now Faustus in the desert trades for gold,
nations acknowledge his peculiar spell;
an utter silence feeds the pride grown old;
respect is mockery and sharpens hell.

The only birds to call this city home
roost on the branching nerves, at every stride
dig talons deeper through the veins' thin crust
to rip the surface of my life's winding dream —
such thoughts as these: I carry Time on my wrist,
a weak thong straps that daemon at my side;
he overshadows me, unseen to others
who only see the hands on a common dial
and not the hands I linked for my undoing
naming Duration, chains of change and decay.
His fingers are ten winds that fan the stars,
extinguish some and set others glowing;
mountains are more impermanent and the forests
wither not much slower than a flower-bed;
their deep-grained iron trunks, supple as stalks
of dandelions to me, his fingers crumple.
Even the land has that old enemy Ocean
quiet as a cat rubbing the edge of things
and purring on the limits of destruction.
The tragedy of human habitations
is subject for the eloquence of Gibbon,
I meditate private disasters only,
and, among these, Time's treachery to women;
the faint cosmetic mask grain by grain stolen
till their moon-faces wane and no light fills
with thin romantic foliage lips' dry valleys.

The root of misery is the fact of change
always anticipated by the mind,
but, met like Dürer's *Death* at a street-crossing,
would shock imagination to create
new forms of permanence and evolve machines
not anthropomorphic but in power like Spring,
whence young gods would step down to wound the earth,
raising like crocus-flocks delicate beings —
as spirits flutter from the gash of pain.

Time the cartographer makes no more quaint maps,
putting at boundaries where venture failed
a whorlëd Kraken belching blank surmise,

but over all, profaning mysteries,
lays sleek meridians crossed with parallels;
so the twin hemispheres Anger and Love,
with forests feathered and wide ocean eyes,
decoyed at mating like wild sea-birds, glare
in gorgeous ruin from the cuckold's net.

    Later, causality builds on this foundation
an iron pain and concrete mass of thought;
such a cuirass as Milton's Satan wanted
against the coldly bright angelic darts,
insinuating hope, remorse, regret,
(slow, dimming poisons), in his sparkling veins.
Emotion sprouts slender geometries,
angular vines and dark festooning cables,
bursting in crackling heads that shed for scent
a sick mauve luminosity in our lanes.
All deathless vegetation frets far off,
the arborescent chaos of the blood
lapping like water the sea-walls of sense;
the womb of words and grave where naked men
not shrouded, sewn and coffined in conceits,
but embryonic corpses of desire,
rock in the moon-drawn cradle of a sea,
warm, dark, salt, secret, turbid, dung-tanged, waste.

I.

When the worn city sets the last task down,
purveying pleasure to flawed fanatic throngs,
and lies still grumbling under a sheet of light,
I come into my room and sit alone;
when the body drowses it is time to think.
We have been chasing fetishes all day,
the city's game, shy secretive gratuities
of passing women and the huge excess
(let us empty our bag out on the floor)
of Flemish goddesses sailing the air
with lumbering buttocks creaming half the sky,
the emanations of innate desire;
and wisps of anguish gathered off the breeze,
malice of petrol, irony of chypre;
immaculate elegance even we bore down
with rites and pomp deep in the sumptuous brain,
archaic luxury of sacrifice
on the worn altar of our self-esteem;
no pavements quavered to the pace of thought
or the hordes flying the approach of thought,
the loutish mass with lingering moonish smiles
on vast cod-faces swimming crowded lanes;
the gamut of the senses roused in us
moods rich in discords, seasonal harmonies
of blossom, of fruition and of dearth
but never the young months' resurgent thrill;
this sack will vomit only dust and feathers
from frantic wings beating into the blue —
the pigments and cosmetics of delight,
the sawdust pool under the daily log
that thins our allotted pile to feed Time's fire.

II.

In shallows of sleep with this litter round us
we lie at the mercy of terror's totems.
The nurslings of nature, necessity's goths,
chalk-faced, stripe-drawn, silvery grotesques,
mercury-hued, like mirrors or metaphors
of destruction, its deeds and unknown dreads,
come marching to cow us from turbulent steppes.
In a landscape we lie, moonlit enough
to open avenues of unavailing woe
and pools of such purity leopards of gold
on the glistening fringes flicker in fear.
Over heath our path runs, with no home or haven,
and with bogs beset, black-scum encrusted.
The keen air, crystalline mask,
gags the gaunt mouth of pride crest-fallen
whose yap is beast-like, but no beast's bellow
thus soars and dwindles in lonely shame
when the reckless rout rollicks behind.

III.
The hunt is up and like a rude
beast the naked soul is gone
out of the world where everyone
wears a protective attitude.

Under the body's pasty hide
rivers flow by globby hills,
ancient Ocean's tawny rills
drench a murderer-suicide;

for the invert's cherished flail
and the lovers' retching kiss
are analogies of this,
like the scorpion's mangled tail.

But the mammals in the street
greet each other with delight,
out of overhanging night
mingle paws and gently bleat.

There the victim with reproach
eyes his dilatory fate,
who 'regrets he should be late',
with solicitous approach.

There is nothing to dispute
since the bargain's drawn and sealed;
but in sleep's vast hunting-field
indeterminate pursuit.

The absence on the sleeping face
denotes all this and something more,
an emblem of the game in store
behind the calm that broods on space.

ASSUAGEMENT
In Covent Garden Market, early

What messages are these the morning brings
my angry city from kind-bosomed fields?
The cool, soft words of vegetable things
placating her whose rumour never yields
to the far-blown persuasion of quiet grass;
whose wrinkled fever dew-fall never cools;
now for a moment stilled, as wagons pass,
to faint remembrance of her ancient pools.

The streets of pain and theatres of despair,
the heart's metropolis, this peace dispute,
matching solidity against permanence;
only the moon wears a consistent air,
watching the clouds answer the winds' thin flute
in azure meadows' pure inheritance.

THEME FOR
THE PSEUDO-FAUSTUS

Faustus, whose high-pitched brow glows in the mirror,
the focus of contemplation, the sacred egg
in which ambition spies the excellent bird
whose parturition shall incinerate
the old world and induce the reign of light,
contrasts the prophecy with circumstance.

    The polar desolation of his state,
ringed-in with streets that tawdry wishes built,
contracts existence to the minimum.
Thought veils as lichen the rock-face of fact
whence of delight the burnished ancient orbs
throw fretful rays, sunk deep in raw-rimmed pits;
free creatures whine, hide and shiver in cellars;
viscid emotions merely, like old women
wrapped against winter stepping into cars,
waddle in sequence from each banal function.
The authoritative world holds him still awed,
its splintering props seem staunch, he hears not
the underworking of its ruinous heirs.

    For Merlin, master of mystery, spell-numbed,
frets in his green grave and the land stirs;
the lawless spirit faith reported chained,
from low regions rises bright as the sky
before the sun puts out the stars; the Serpent,
casting his sheath, re-diamonded, lifts
the flat axe head against love's wounding heel.
Pride, mobilised in swift sub-human hosts,
the lithe and predatory thought of joy,
invests the earth; but Faustus in his deep dump
doubts of damnation and whimpers to his glass:
'The holy egg is addled: we grow old:
there is nothing on earth to do, we are outside life.
Throw up the window? Or throw up the sponge?'

    The golden figure of light strides through dawn fields,
the furrowed cloud-land yields the acrid sun;
Morning's thin air floods the streets like fresh blood

in sacrifice to the now-imminent pain,
so all our slaughtered desires take heart to rise
and lip life's puddle in the dissolving gloom.
The gluey envelope of being swirls
like ink in water and the senses' suit
soon tears to scarecrow flesh whose flapping rags
warn blind earth of certain hovering beaks.
The *I* is bodiless and, a mere stripped nerve
steeped in the culture of aseptic light,
throbs to the rhythm of the lilting rays.
The human concept like a shrivelled husk
rasps its complaint even on the breeze of hope:
'This air is spirit's blood, at every breath
ten generations die, but we remounting
through organisations now remote and stiff
to the quick vigour of the early men,
find no home-comforts by the primitive hearth.
Cock of the midden or flairing garbage-cans,
our brief dawn-crow is muffled in the wet
blanket of history; like a leching frog
caught in mid-rapture under the world's vast turd
we jerk exhausted limbs in endless folds;
and stifling, spitting, furiously frustrated,
perish, not budging, with intense exertion.'

   This too-rare atmosphere flays the slow flesh,
eye-crystals crackle and the racked nerves smart,
sharp tides of pain invade and strain the heart,
oceans of tears sway before us till the blood
blots out that desert sea with its warm stream;
and the *I* retreating down familiar paths
rears its defence against the terrible sun
and in its figurative way rebuilds
the altar and brothel of legitimate state
adjacent, with mean fanes darkening our streets:
the silver-swimming gutters blench and fade
to sinks and sewers where tarnished spirits lap,
obscenely supine, the stale brink of day.

   The demonstrable world remains, whose hordes advance
when wagons over cobbles beat the march
for hurrying feet to gain counter or bench,

and the vague faces query, as they flow,
the pavements, placards, windows for a sign.
Deprived of freedom in time, space and love
they seek enfranchisement in the air beyond
the city's silent rows of gnawing roofs,
expecting joy within the mouth of doom;
drab rotting leaves on life's prevailing wind,
in pain and pleasure glued woman to man,
even in the grave's foul bed — or headstones lie.

   Damned by foreknowledge, in the crowded hall
the tedious programme promises no end,
heaping fresh items in successive pain,
whirlpools and cataracts of scathing sound,
the sores and running ulcers that consume
the womb of silence and night's patient breast,
unless new instruments evoke release;
the sabotage of all the delicate tools,
the swift insidious wheels, the quiet machines
where the cramped mind weaves endless slave-designs;
the massacre of all the innocent shapes
with tendril-clinging arms and pulpy lips,
bastards of hand-grips, spawn of self-distrust;
the desecration of ideal desire;
the violation of the veiled design;
repudiation and the doom of pride,
the death-dance on the tight-rope of the will
taut over chaos crammed with serried masks;

naked, and balanced on the brooding void.

THE HAPPY NEW YEAR

A Masque

We are thought meete of all men whom agayn
Should hugy heap of Chaos overly
And world oppresse with overturned masse.
The latest age now falleth us upon,
With evil hap we are begot alas.
If, wretches, we have lost the sight of sonne,
Or him by fraught enforced have to flye,
Let our complaints yet goe and fear be past:
He greedy is of life that will not die
When all the world shall end with him at last.

> Jasper Heywood, translating
> Seneca's *Thyestes*

Dramatis Personae

THE PRESENTER
CHORUS OF NEUTERS OR PHILOSOPHERS
SINISTERS   DEXTERS

Dances by

THE LEBANON GIRLS
THE FRAZER EIGHT

The Action spans a Solar Year.

Out of a livid sunrise the iron face of Sol
emerges rusty from night-deep ocean,
Sol the Deliverer!
The cloud-white fingers grip cold peaks
to hoist him from his hoary solitude
over the Eastern hill.
Rosy-slippered dawn
goes tripping down the spangled lawns
but drab reminders dun insolvent streets.
Elegant hyacinthine light-plants shed
perpetual brilliance through long wards
where moribund the later sons of earth
bask and chew up remainders of their days,
contemning Sol's archaic ways
whose heaped bonfire in the romantic style
nurtures their candle-end of wit and wisdom.
Like an old bard the shaggy sire of song
batters in vain on supercilious brows,
the wall-eyed city, blinking steel and stone,
spits back his bounty in the monarch's eye.

CHORUS

O poor old man! Poor good old man!
To shame the silver cloud-locks thus!

PRESENTER

Tungsten tears matted the tawny beard.

CHORUS

Majesty outraged sheds a cosmic blight.

PRESENTER

Sol reels heavily homeward no more facing faithless,
sharper than serpents' teeth,
misbegotten, whoreson earth-defilers, kites.

CHORUS

O now is doomsday, now the shut of eve,
and the small rain comes down.

PRESENTER

The slope of winter, declivity of eld.

Sol falls weakly through his ruined house,
a dead coal in a rusty grate —

Sad visitation of old enthusiasms!

PRESENTER
past splintered floor-boards and cold empty hearths
of heaven, whence drifts the thin grey ashen rain,
the burnt-out proclamations of false stars.
Dupes dither by Thames brook
of vows rescinded, broken contracts, hordes
renounce complaint in wan waters, some
fall on pity's sword and heap up
lapfuls of bowels in ostentatious arms.

CHORUS
London has many merciful instruments.

PRESENTER
These withered souls pluck themselves off,
the dead king's cortège drifting underlands
with bands of music wailing through the streets.

(*Here the* SINISTERS *come on.*)

PRESENTER
The choirs of sorrow congregate
with broken voices on banks
of metropolitan streams,
and rasping litanies unclench
into the sombre sky.

Sucked up by ragged clouds, their groans
leave the streets emptier; the arcs
stutter with pride, their lethal light
flings pallor on these masks,
joy-seekers in night's maze.

Doors gape but none goes home,
ghosts planted in their beds
dig in sharp roots

watered with sweat of memories,
love's vigorous tears;

and long dank heads pending
broke-necked from upper windows
like ducks from poulterers' slabs,
wake deathly last-Spring thoughts —

CHORUS
O ineluctable pendulums!

SINISTERS
Wounds got in many wars,
(time heals all hurts, they say)
but Mars' and Venus' scars
still sign our flesh today,
got under those bright stars
as they in conjunction lay.

We crowd midnight pavement
brilliant as arctic noon
though the crammed firmament
denies us any boon;
for the stars' thin dole is spent,
we are overdrawn on the moon.

Like old weapons we rust
under the biting air,
and if we desire it is just
to wrap us from all this care
in our sheet of disgust
and our blanket of despair.

CHORUS
The quiet engines of the air
weave and unweave in dull routine
bright hangings on the hooks of care
and make of rocks a restful scene.

The anxious generations climb
from peak to peak and all their pay
a soft shroud at the end of time
of wind, rain, shadow and decay.

80

(The scene is blotted out.)

SINISTERS

Numbed hands implore no more,
the dark is cold, His passing left
open a door behind our back;
a starless wind
blots out our warmth and light:
this is the world's night.

*(There is a pause during which the scene becomes
slowly visible again.)*

PRESENTER

A fog-like poison drifts and whirls
such dreadful faces as the sun shone on
lying in fields, propped against walls, on beds
mottled with leaf-lights,
blotched bladders, craving eyes,
float swarming fast in gulfs
below the roots of tombs and claws of churchyard trees,
below the tubes and drains and creeping cable,
deeper is only fire.

CHORUS

but then the forest and tideless air of fable.

PRESENTER

Sol gropes in warm womb midnight
softer than velvet sheath,
the embryo-ancient,
tearless, toneless, timeless, unaware
what silken currents drag his lair.

SINISTERS

Slow patterns flow on walls
dimly responsive, underseas
of waving fronds that pasture yet
leviathan hungers, and excite
vague luxuries not deed nor word:

an abstract pageant, gorgeous forms
of qualities not known nor named

81

F

till birth-break and the clank
of turning keys — the prisoner-child
fling open all those cells.

Long files of promises held up
by winter's white hand wait
with musics stilled, not dumb,
to burst along our streets
subduing want and loss.

DEXTERS
(heard but not seen)
We doze behind our felted doors
through the long season of doubt,
till Sol knock with reviving power
enticing flesh to venture out.

But turn again till Sol be fit
to furnish plain men's needs —
a world new-stocked with mates and meat,
good dreams and simple deeds.

PRESENTER
Sol climbs weakly through his furbished house,
the infant watery eyes light on
bare walls whose fresh-hung skins of imagery
show cornucopias swollen huge with seed,
the abstract and fair promise of abundance.
Sky-watchers raised in quaking towers of hope
see the bold child lurch to the Fishes' room
and prophesy mountains of incredible spawn
to stuff the seven seas of human want.

CHORUS
Coax and cajole him with words soft as sighs
and leafy toys easing day's long slope.

PRESENTER
In Lebanon the blood-red rain,
and moaning girls limping like wounded doves
who bear his gardens to the bleeding streams —
their little pot-clay Edens, mimic groves

of fresh-plucked twigs that symbolise desire
swift-withering on the edge of expectation,
and cast with both hands on the impetuous current
implore assuagement and burden of fruition.
    (*The* LEBANON GIRLS *in mute accompaniment.*)

CHORUS

Urge him with antic gestures step by step,
and mask the features of ancestral spleen.

PRESENTER

Fantastic ceremonial floods the world.
Some swing all day between their orchard trees,
some light bonfires, leaping through the flames,
some burst through hoops, and others beat the woods
to seize the green man with the snow-white poll
where he runs wild, and drag him to the village,
for power hung hostage above the chimney-place.
    (*The* FRAZER EIGHT *in illustrative acrobatics.*)

PRESENTER

Obsequious ritual bends the flaming will:
Sol rides in triumph through Metropolis.

CHORUS

How like a prince visiting his chief city,
and all benevolence, he scatters gold!
Even the surliest suburbs cheer him in!

PRESENTER

Quotidian streets sparkle like paths to fame.

CHORUS

Light is a bugle whipping the numbed nerves
with cords of brass.

PRESENTER
                    The sunny side of the road
crawls with the aged like a lousy seam.

CHORUS

The parasites lift up what hearts they have.

83

An embryo with dim reptilian brain
womb-bound in Wandsworth, and the female flocks
from dullest Kensington, and City ants,
and owl-wise Bloomsbury, all send up a shout.

CHORUS
The wide globe swims in milky seas of bliss!

PRESENTER
Now blond rays stroke the flesh,
the viridescent Park
is populous Eden. Sleek-flanked Eve
woos carefree Adam.

CHORUS
That forbidden Tree
spreads not in the accessible inane.

SINISTERS
Then fetters soft as daisy-chains
bound day to day with puerile joys —
now goat turds blot our fragrant toys
and morning herds us to the trains.

Even today we child-men, led
by mild eyes, seek those tender bonds,
but the goat's old-man's cough responds
from pleasure's solitary bed.

DEXTERS *bound on, and troll lustily:*
We do not crave eternity,
love's bowl of quintessential pearl,
since half an hour's propinquity
exhausts the meaning of a curl,
but hail one Blessed Trinity,
the Time, the Place and a Girl.

Bland tyrants of the lifted skirt,
we straddle dizzy gulfs of doubt,
compunction and the mere inert,
for mind is staunch, the member stout;

and the male impulse we assert
sows blind the seed whence heroes sprout.

The starry heaven is a sponge
our ardour has compressed and dried,
yet still through empty dark we lunge
seeking the soft, complaisant side
for consummation, when we plunge
in velvet depths our rigid pride.

CHORUS
The flaming god hangs down his head
on locks begummed with mutual zest,
but nightly by fresh vigour fed
shall rise again to stand the test.

And every dawn for faithful crowds
convoked by Earth to sumptuous strife,
old Sol shall spurt through spermy clouds
his scarlet face, the seed of life.

(*Here the* DEXTERS *join with the* LEBANON GIRLS
and mime their fancy.)

SINISTERS
The shadows that the old year knew
in the winter of its care,
are melted and the world made new.

Link arms and twist the vine-wreaths in your hair,
Dexters and Girls, you happy norms
guess not our frontiers nor the brunt we bear.

New blood begets new forms
for comedies or tragic shows,
new vigour to confront old storms.

So for your play's last set propose
Time and Eternity are one;
thought shall not function through our toes,
we will assent till this short dance be done.

(*Here a general dance. Then the stage empties.*)

PRESENTER

Unctuous with toil well done,
a ruddy, sweating mask,
the heavenly Ploughman
now plods through cloud-barred fields
slanting a last mild smile
on the town's thick-sown furrows
ripening to harvest,
whence the dextrous couples
hitched fast by votive bonds
shall draw Time's toppling wain
to all-men's Harvest Home.

CHORUS

Like begets like, immortal in each kind;
through perishing units' union, death's defeat.

PRESENTER

I see others who walk the earth tonight, homeless
throughout the city, pacing day's void suburbs
by unmade roads, raw gardens, blank-eyed lamps,
cinders and tin-cans and blown evening papers,
among refuse-pits and sewer-mouths,
wandering fires and voices of the swamp;
passing deliberately into the night
through the infinite extension of this landscape,
with thoughts like pilgrims' staves they picked their way
to a lucid zone, whence fresh horizons blazed.

Orchestra

PROVINCIAL NIGHTPIECE

When girls return from tennis on
slim bicycles of hollow steel
through their veins' colder channels steal
the sentiments of Tennyson.

Those censers of impurity
infect the air with vulgar dreams
of lovers by exclusive streams
and plages of rich fatuity.

Or otherwise they long to bear
ten children to some honest John;
content, whilst he is getting on,
to darn and patch their underwear.

In cardboard hats and plastic shoes
and art-silk impudence they glide,
all substitute. Could beauty ride
Godiva-like, and use no ruse?

The Proustian idyll's flowering grove
was blighted by poor key-hole Tom:
purdah's drawn blinds had saved us from
the forward vision blasting love.

Yet I have bedded, I protest,
the paragon of elegance;
when Night with his star-dripping lance
feathered our solipsistic nest.

Tonight the casual moon looks down
with more indifference than before
on pimp and parson, prude and whore,
those shadows in a dead town;

thus my cold thought lights up the scene,
by virtue of a distant sun,
from whose frozen vigour none
may plead desire shall intervene.

Only the ardour of the past,
that once embraced with arms of flame
these shapes my brain can hardly name
now, holds this decor fast.

Those are the figures fancy bred
to people voids behind the eyes;
but hard facts revolutionise
the population of the head.

When dawn shall tear our sky to rags,
and trams, the tumbrils of revolt,
crash down with every cherished dolt,
red laughter waving maddening flags;

love's *ci-devants* all driven-in
shall pay our private rancour's debts;
and soon the *rigor mortis* sets
each bashed face in a Christ-like grin;

as shams and shibboleths collapse
swift forms replenish our tired earth,
of bouncing goddesses and mirth-
mad gods with wine-and-oil smeared chaps.

DIVAGATION ON A LINE OF DONNE'S

My verse the strict map of my misery . . .

But by the trigonometry of wit
canalised into those luxuriant tracts
where monsters of imaginative pride
writhe in the harsh nets of Scholastic writ.

That tangled growth of intellect and passion,
where thought spread sensuous, mental love's last acts,
where doubt's exuberance even doubt defied,
thrust skywards in the noon-day of ambition.

Till in a flash which humbled that rich Earth
Donne saw Time's handiwork on the bodies of men,
and Death, squat in each wrinkle as a trench,
sniping the careless heads of Love and Mirth.

He wooed God 'like an angel from a cloud',
preaching; but sometimes the more faithful pen
revived a metaphor that had trapped a wench
and shames the dandy in the wimpled shroud.

ODE TO A TRAIN-DE-LUXE
Written on a railway embankment near London
and inscribed to our public idealists

On your sprung seats the Faithful glide
oblivious of the world that is,
O Pullmans where we never ride
to Brightons of remoter bliss!

We watch, our bowels gripped hard with spleen,
your soft, luxurious passing-by.
Do glass and varnish so serene
repudiate no human cry?

How like successful businessmen
at ease your travellers sit and stare!
Perhaps such phlegm is natural when
one sees Relations as they Are?

They seem to one another's gaze
mighty adventurers at least,
having reached Truth by devious ways,
though without rising from their seats.

Far from the city, grossly real,
through Nature's Absolute they stroll,
and nimbly chase the untamed Ideal
through palm-courts of the *Metropole*.

Rapt in familiar unison
with God, whose face must soon appear,
they show their wife and eldest son
the fat-cheeked moon rise, from the Pier.

And we, too, with as little fuss,
might thus ignore the world's dark edge,
but those dead rays to coatless us
augur the thin end of time's wedge.

What rocket-plane shall pierce this fate
and hurl us past doom-destined space
where we might found the virile state,
Pious Aeneas of the skyward Race?

Delusion theirs'; ours' duty. Choice,
suspended, eyes the dense star-ranks;
yet, Sirened, leans to your husky voice,
O Dido-city on Thames' banks!

TWITTINGPAN
AND SOME OTHERS

Twittingpan seized my arm, though I'd have gone
willingly. To be seen with him alone,
the choicest image of the present age,
flattered my vanity into quite a rage.
His was the presence always in dispute
by every cocktail hostess of repute;
and I'd long enjoyed seeing his drooping form
breast each successive new-aesthetic storm.
He had championed Epstein, Gertrude, and *Parade*,
and even now was nothing of a die-hard;
(I had last heard him on some Red-film show-day
expounding *tonal montage* in the foyer);
being two days nimbler than the smartest clique
he gave the cachet to the safest chic.
      We turned from Regent Street to Conduit Street.
He thought my overcoat was far from neat,
offered his tailor's name and then forgot.
His mind was in a turmoil and overshot
immediate objects in transcendent aims.
Juggling voluptuously with Christian names
he listed for me each new partnership
contracted since I'd given Town the slip
for ten days in the wilds near Sevenoaks;
and Lord! I thought, no wonder Douglas[1] croaks
imminent fire and brimstone; though no Prudhomme,
I could never quite regret the fate of Sodom.
      This intellectual athlete then began
praising the freedom of the modern man
from dogma, morals, and the plagues of nature —
a scientific, half-angelic creature,
immune from all — my hero almost winces —
Tokyo is down,[2] but dancing's on at Prince's.
He summed up briefly all religion means
and then explained the universe by Jeans.
Burly Jack Haldane next supplied his text
(and as the Sacred Writ is always vext
into queer meanings for sectarian ends),
Twittingpan preached the marriage of true friends
when blessed parthenogenesis arrives
and he-uranians can turn honest wives.

'Consider Bond Street,' as we reached it, cried
falsetto Twittingpan our period's pride,
'Does it not realise in microcosm
the whole ideal Time nurses in its bosom?
Luxury, cleanliness and objets d'art,
the modern Trinity for us all who are
freed from the burden of the sense of sin.
Lord Russell says . . . ' I feared he would begin
an exposition of the free man's worship,
that neo-anabaptist, compelled to dip
not now from mystic but hygienic motives.
'But look, in Shanks's[3] shop the Past still lives;
those gross utensils symbolically bind us
to the brute part we soon shall leave behind us,
for Haldane promises in the world-to-come
excretion's inoffensive minimum.'[4]
He gestured freely and drew inquiring stares
from elegant shoppers wrapped like dainty bears,
whilst I blushed like a country cousin come
to the Time-metropolis from an archaic home.
He saw my red cheeks and with kindly air
proclaimed sophistication everywhere.
'You must meet Iris, she who lives serene
in the intense confession of the obscene
and drags her tea-time sex-affair all fresh
to the dinner-table, like a cat with flesh.
Her new book is, I hear, just too, *too* topical,
though Janet's peeved not to be in it at all.
But Basil's poems are far more utter than
you can imagine, as you don't know the man.'
With that he handed me a deckled sheet
where these lines staggered on uncertain feet:

    you the one onely
    not more but one than
    two is superfluous two is
    i reminds you of me
    me reminds i of you
    i is another
    identify unidentifiable
    then say is love not
    the word

all love is perhaps no love
or is perhaps luck
or no luck is no love rather.

'Chaste, isn't it? And yes, I must explain
that I inspired it, at risk of seeming vain;
otherwise you might miss its fine notations
which do convey so subtly my relations
with the dear fellow. You two must really meet;
he would impress you even in the street.'
I fixed my look at 'silent admiration'
and paced along all tense with expectation,
though bashful at my Siamese-like linking
with the lank oracle of modern thinking.
    'Lewis and Middleton Murry are, I'm sure,
the only moderns likely to endure
of the older crowd; for Eliot's later works
are merely sanctimonious quips and quirks;
and Huxley is portentously obsessed
with the problems that make City clerks depressed.
Don't you think Wyndham Lewis too divine?
That brute male strength he shows in every line!
I swear if he'd flogged me in his last book but one,
as some kind person informed me he has done,
I'd have forgiven him for the love of art.
And you, too, ought to take his works to heart
as I have done, for torn by inner strife,
I've made him mentor of my mental life.
You cannot imagine what a change that worked.
I who was all emotion, and always shirked
the cold chaste isolation of male mind,
now thrust in front all I had kept behind.
I'd lived in Time and Motion and Sensation,
then smashed my watch and burnt the Bloomsbury *Nation*...
But here comes Clarence, — Clarence with Basil!' So
like a hot poker then he let my arm go;
and, stifling jealousy, hailed them with 'How nice!'
They flaunted gay shirts and a grand old vice.
Poor Twittingpan had no novelty to produce;
I was not shabby enough to be of use
as a quaint genius, nor smart enough for friend.
Poor wretch! To put his agony at an end

96

I touched my hat, *good-day, sir*-ed, like a tout,
and left my Twittingpan to lie it out.

[1] James, not Norman. A vice-hound and high-brow baiter employed by the *Sunday Express*.

[2] This refers to the 1923 catastophe. Also to Voltaire.

[3] Sanitary engineers.

[4] See *Daedalus*.

G

THE CONTEMPORARY MUSE
After reading an Anthology of the work of about three hundred living poets

'What thing did I love that walks the street
on limping, foul, and garish-leathered feet?
A simpering, baby-faced suburban trull
come up to Town to find the fools more dull
than in her native Wimbledon, and bent
on turning an honest pound to pay her rent.
And I, damned wretch, once glamoured by her smile,
trailed her sad buttocks nearly half a mile;
her drained and sodden flesh where Browning heaved
spasmodic vows which impotence believed;
and Tennyson laboured all a vernal day
crowning a snotty brat Queen o' the May;
but that was in her middle prime, and now
she's milked of favours easily as a cow,
whilst through a turnstile all her lovers wend,
checked by tired critics at the further end.

'Shall I go through the list from A to Z,
or shall we, sweetheart, take a trip to bed?'
'Why stir the wasps that rim Fame's luscious pot?
Love costs us nothing, satire costs a lot!'

ANSWER TO AN INVITATION TO LOVE DELAYED IN THE POST

But having run so long in grooves of hate,
beaten the bounds of metre choked with spleen;
desired, despaired, despised, and in-between
flattered mere melancholy for a Fate;
we dodge affliction in a shell-fish state;
though rumours reach us of a might-have-been
and suspect messages from joys not seen,
a re-creation seems a shade too late.

Observe a hermit-crab unhoused of gloom
writhe to the scalpels of ecstatic light —
would that become your doyen criticaster
whose yawn blasts true-love's Film on its first night?
Must we grow raw again, emerge, and boom
some world-sweetheart's aureoled disaster?

It seems a cheerless joke
   to have survived—
not wholly ghost nor folk,
   but rarefied.

I stress my old advice
   and the same stave
fits the heart's new device,
   My bed my grave.

And that, my luscious bit
   of loving-stuff,
for woman's nimble wit
   should be enough.

FROM VERLAINE
(Chansons pour Elle. No. xviii.)

If you'd really like, delicious Ignoramus,
I'll act as though my only leaning now were
to paw you up and down (and who could blame us?)
with the expert touch of the utter bounder;
if you'd really like me to, sweet Ignoramus.

So let's be shocking and throw off all constraint,
like girl and doctor in the Freudian clinics.
Send Modesty packing, that old moral taint;
even play up a bit, and though no cynics,
yet let's be shocking and throw off all constraint.

But mind! no bookish talk. Damn the whole trade,
publishers first and foremost! So, desist!
Yield to each impulse of the way we're made,
blissfully ignorant decencies exist;
and mind, no bookish talk! Damn the whole trade!

To do and sleep, our programme. Does that suit you?
There lies our primary and ultimate function;
in that consists our single-double virtue;
sole knowledge and soul-guidance in conjunction;
to do and sleep! Sweetheart, does that suit you?

THE LOUSY ASTROLOGER'S PRESENT
TO HIS SWEETHEART

No Austin-Seven at my door
love's chariot was, but jolting trams
with butts and spittle on the floor
conveyed your peerless hams.

I could not buy great gems to rest
like moons or blood against your flesh,
nor softly cloud your moonlight breast
in silken, star-shot mesh.

I owned no marble throne to raise
your grace above the stumbling crowd;
no vast horned herds had I at graze
to make your passion proud.

But a spontaneous species browsed
the bosky pasture of my groins,
begotten when great Sol caroused
in Taurus and my loins.

These, my sole subject creatures, thrive
beneath majestic thumb-nail law.
All mildly live and kindly wive,
except the glutton jaw.

So for the tribute Beauty drew,
outflowering from her calyx, frock,
I could pay but one pregnant ewe,
The fairest of that flock.

She: More eager than a sun-drunk bee,
that pet so cherished for your sake
clings at the very root of me
and sucks its nurse awake.

He: From this forced watching of the stars
we may the better judge our fate,
and learn if past these sensual jars
our inmost selves may mate.

From the vexed House the Crab controls,
see! our twin destinies remove,
and reach as manumitted souls
the Balance of true love.

She: Sky-ecstasies seem so austere,
Dearest! my novice ardour fails.
Can't we assay love's richness here?
Let my breast be the Scales!

THE HANDMAID OF RELIGION

'The writers of books, the painters of pictures, the actors for the stage or on the screen, the women by the fashion of their dress, who render self-control more difficult for the average normal man or woman . . . are doing moral evil.'

THE CARDINAL ARCHBISHOP OF WESTMINSTER

'I am, as is perhaps well known, a Protestant. But I am quite sure that these words will be concurred in by the heads of my own Church and by the heads of the great Nonconformist Churches.'

THE HOME SECRETARY, VISCOUNT BRENTFORD

Dear Queenie, though it breaks my heart,
I fear that you and I must part,
in case we sink too deep in sin,
I for my verse, you for your skin —
I mean the double envelope
that rouses, and confirms, our hope —
you sack, whose rose-leaf wrappings hide
what harsh Tertullian specified!
Here lies the parting of our ways,
and once again the woman pays:
the vows of Art I can abjure
and save my soul in shoddy rhyme,
but, stripped, your beauty would endure,
no less a sin, in fact a crime.
One article your harsher code
admits, to save you actual flaying —
to choose some unbecoming mode,
but that, I fear, is past obeying.

Poor girl, but such is moral law,
expounded without any flaw;
and to your harm I must confess
you have an artist's touch in dress:
for in the squalor of the crowd,
dull replicas, or grossly loud,
when you pass by, men's average eyes
gleam with a spark I recognise.
They glimpse a moment other lives,
including, doubtless, other wives,

and with this dim idea of beauty
return disturbed to home and duty,
where but for you the docile soul
might rot in perfect self-control.

I have a much more complex task,
and seven sins I must unmask,
lurking disguised in every line
to snatch my reader's soul and mine;
for, though our moralists annex
all blame to the one sin of sex,
Churchmen, when manners were more genial,
found fleshly lapses almost venial;
at least when measured side by side
with sins of spiritual pride;
but now it's safer to blaspheme
than to revive a classic theme.

Even Jix, that stalwart in theology,
reduces history to pornology,
with one stroke of a master-mind
leaves Gibbon limping far behind,
and reconstructs the fall of Rome
from recent goings-on at home.
Neither barbarians nor malaria
destroyed Rome's grip on her vast area,
but naughty novels sold in shops
unhindered by censorious cops.*

Since perfect form is what inspires
Mind with unquenchable desires,
and in the Dionysian rage
Flesh strides an ampler, braver stage,
the arts, perhaps, are more obscene
than Jix or Bourne can even mean,
whose dicta echo one another's
like any spiritual brothers'.†

*'I suppose nothing contributed more to the degradation of the Roman Empire
than the stream of pernicious literature which flowed like an open sewer through
that great city.' (Viscount Brentford)
†'There are other matters in life of greater importance than the free development
of a particular form of Art.'(The Viscount) 'No silly prating . . . that the claims
of Art must be satisfied.' (The Cardinal)

But as we both must earn our bread,
and such as they are still our head,
my Queenie, let us now conform,
and so ride out the impending storm;
for who would risk their job, and hell,
for dressing, or for writing, well?

Since Beauty's famous 'single hair'
seems planned a comprehensive snare,
(Wise Providence! Perverted Man!)
we will be sluttish as we can.
I will compete with tedious Quarles
whilst you subdue the infants' squalls;
and in our bed, only at need,
we will such normal monsters breed —
their tendency to misbehaving
purged of all aesthetic craving —
as must, for this wise Prelate's part,
be supreme arbiters of Art.

LES MARTYRS D'AUJOURD'HUI
(Vide: Freud's *Totem and Tabu*)

'The Crucifixion is an Incest Myth,
Christ's blood procures our well-earned doom's reprieve.
It needs intelligence', claimed Mr Smythe,
'to know such things, yet, childlike, still believe.

'We cherish simple faith, though it offend
the saturnalia of this modern Rome.
Good Friday night my wife and I attend
A Sacred Concert in the Hippodrome.'

A GLIMPSE INTO THE GREAT BEYOND
(Sir Arthur Conan Doyle is reported to have held several conversations, since his decease, with Mr Hannen Swaffer.)

Now that Sir Arthur has the run
of all the pleasures Space can offer,
might we conclude they're not much fun
since he comes back to talk to Swaffer?

AN OLD RHYME RE-RHYMED

'But our lot crawls between dry ribs
To keep our metaphysics warm.'
                                    T. S. Eliot

Those who are much obsessed by death
and see the skull beneath the skin,
may cheat their fear of wanting breath
with dry philosophy or gin;

or with the ardours of the birch
or lure of buxom female form,
but whose lot creeps into the Church
to keep its inhibitions warm?

HINTS FOR MAKING A GENTLEMAN
Sans Peur et sans Reproche

Maintain the schoolboy's simple faith
in the good God who gave him breath,
and fashioned earth for his delight
by Hebrew myth and natural right!
Let library shelves sustain from reach
the facts experience may teach;
and Swift and Schopenhauer be banned
past grasp of most inquiring hand;
such pessimists are all suspect
for they might teach him to correct
the blind insurgent ego-lust
that goads this paladin of dust
and gives him in his rage for pelf
rule of all creatures but himself;
whose ignorance makes him strong to die
quite admirably for a lie —
as might have been observed in Flanders,
at least in subaltern commanders.

But long before he's ripe for slaughter
he's after his house-master's daughter:
so in the rut of sport divert
this native tendency to flirt,
though he evolve as equipoise
an interest in the smaller boys;
for this preserves our womanhood
intacta, and his thirst for blood.

When even the debauch of games
can't wean him from the need of dames,
he'll learn what women he may use
to ease his hypertrophied thews.
These, though not socially alive,
are visited from twelve till five,
when in the Eden of their rooms
as Adam he a moment blooms;

though in broad daylight and the street
he must forget them if they meet;
since courtesy is in good taste
only if it is not a waste:
and gentlemen made on this plan
are an efficient type of man —
knowing with inborn certitude
to whom they can be safely rude.

    His purely intellectual gifts
(assisted by mnemonic shifts),
in course of time grow fit to deal
with all the problems known as real:
as, what opinions to express
about the subjects in the Press;
on moral judgements, whóm consider
a pukka sahib or outsider,
where right and wrong is closely knit
with schools and clubs and clothes that fit —
a system louts throw out of gear
who flaunt gay ties they'd dare not wear
if only Britain's legislators
would rally to our alma maters.*

    Now, if the City is his goal,
he's rendered fit to take control;
and, with high precepts long imbued,
graces that seat of rectitude,
and markets now absorb his brain,
with only golf to ease the strain.

    So launched upon the sea of life
he comes in time to take a wife,
whom he must choose with all the care
of an old farmer at a Fair:
her flesh and brain must show like brands
all the ideals for which he stands —
persistence in the social path;

*And impose penalties on those who wear the ties of schools to which they never
belonged, as advocated in letters to the *Daily Telegraph*.

the habit of a frequent bath.
In private she need not disown
certain opinions of her own:
for all men like their mares high-mettled;
but till the ancient question's settled,
which of our various creeds is true,
she must do what the others do
and go to Church, though not too often,
like one whose mind is really open.
With social service in the air
and helpers needed everywhere
she might be one of those who spend
an afternoon in the East End
spreading like gospels in the masses
the culture of the upper classes.
For nursing mothers 'Sexual Ethics',
for half-crown tarts 'The New Athletics';
and justify by such tuition
the privileges of position.

   Then when the happy moment dawns
and his bride blushing through her lawns
like the sun melting clouds asunder
fills him with ecstasy and wonder —
he knows it's quite a different thrill
from what he got with Fanny Hill,
and swears to no more lay his head
on pillows of a hired bed,
when he by sacred joys may come,
and safer pleasures, in the home.

   Thirty or forty years of this
induces spiritual bliss;
and in his life's declining glow
the Scheme of Things begins to show.

   He sees that Providence must share
his own idea of what is fair
since he's lived some score years in comfort
without the slightest mental effort
whilst men of almost equal talent
whole lives in fruitless struggle spent.

So bravely watching death approach,
as free from fear as self-reproach,
he rightly trusts that he may save
his sense of values in the grave;
for as the body muckward sinks
it still lacks sense to tell he stinks.

H

TO THE WIFE OF A
NON-INTERVENTIONIST
STATESMAN

TO THE WIFE OF A
NON-INTERVENTIONIST STATESMAN
(March 1938)

Permit me, Madam, to invade,
briefly, your boudoir's pleasant shade.
Invade? No, that's entirely wrong!
I volunteered, and came along.
So please don't yell, or make a scene,
or ring for James to — intervene.
I'm here entirely for the good
of you and yours, it's understood.
No ballyhoo, what I've to say
may stand you in good stead one day.

    I have to broach a matter that
less downright folk might boggle at,
but none need blush because we try
to analyse the marriage tie.

    The voice that breathed o'er Eden laid
some precepts down to be obeyed:
to seek in marriage mutual trust
much more than sentiment or lust:
to base our passion on esteem
and build a home for love's young dream.
With this in mind, I'll state a case
of interest to the human race.

    Suppose a husband yarns in bed
of plans that fill his lofty head,
think what should be a wife's reaction
if he turned out the tool of faction,
who put across the crooked schemes
of statesmen sunk in backward dreams;
whose suave compliance sealed the fate
of thousands left to Franco's hate —
(those very Basques whose fathers drowned
to keep *our* food-ships safe and sound,
sweeping for mines in furious seas).
Our Fleet stood by, but ill at ease:
restive, our sailors watched the shore

whilst hundreds drowned who'd starved before,
victims of Franco's sham blockade —
though in the way of honest trade
Potato Jones and his brave lass
had proved this husband knave or ass.

Suppose he argues: Though I swerved
from honour's course, yet peace is served?

Euzkadi's mines supply the ore
to feed the Nazi dogs of war:
Guernika's thermite rain transpires
in doom on Oxford's dreaming spires:
in Hitler's frantic mental haze
already Hull and Cardiff blaze,
and Paul's grey dome rocks to the blast
of air-torpedoes screaming past.
From small beginnings mighty ends,
from calling rebel generals friends,
from being taught at public schools
to think the common people fools,
Spain bleeds, and England wildly gambles
to bribe the butcher in the shambles.

Traitor and fool's a combination
to lower wifely estimation,
although there's not an Act in force
making it grounds for a divorce:
but canon law forbids at least
cohabitation with a beast.

The grim crescendo rises still
at the Black International's will.
Mad with the loss of Teruel
the bestial Duce looses hell;
on Barcelona slums he rains
German bombs from Fiat planes.
Five hundred dead at ten a second
is the world record so far reckoned;
a hundred children in one street,
their little hands and guts and feet,
like offal round a butcher's stall,
scattered where they were playing ball —

117

because our ruling clique's pretences
rob loyal Spain of its defences,
the chaser planes and ack-ack guns
from which the prudent Fascist runs.

　　So time reveals what people meant
who framed a Gentleman's Agreement,
and lest a final crime condones
fresh massacres with British loans,
should not its sponsor be outlawed
from power, position, bed and board?
Would not a thinking wife contemn
the sneaking hand that held the pen
and with a flourish signed the deed
whence all these hearts and bodies bleed?
Would not those fingers freeze the breast
where the young life should feed and rest?
Would not his breath reek of the tomb
and with cold horror seal her womb?
Could a true woman bear his brat?
No need to answer!
　　　　　　　　　　Thanks, my hat.

LATER VERSES
AND A DIVERSION

HOW NIKOLAI GOGOL
FAILED TO SAVE HIS SOUL

Scenario

Gogol took pride in his creations, thus
offending God, as his Father confessor warned him;
and he made Gogol purge his sin by hard penance.
But ever and again there came seeping, as it were,
through his lacerated flesh the green ghost of a tulip.
And Gogol shivered, feeling himself irrevocably
adjudged to the eternal hell of frost and ice
so that he shivered on his blanketless bed,
wafer thin and felt the backbone through his belly,
in unendurable penance.
In the ghastly depths of his despair
his own creatures danced sarabands before his eyes.
If Nikolai could create living beings, had he not
a foot on the ladder to the Divine?
'A ladder quick!' faint words unheeded.

Voice of Father Mathew

'Nikolai Vasilevich, where do you hide now?
In the cold stove, among the ashes of your blasphemous
  creations still defiling you?
Come back quickly that I may purge you with penances.'
Reluctantly obedient, the spirit rears from the stove.
Yet Father Mathew was at many versts distance.
Whence then this docility?
Yet the horror of eternal damnation still shook Gogol's
almost fleshless form.
The leeches sucked with blind fury, but no blood came.
'A ladder' he moans, 'a ladder'.
Had not his foot conquered the first rung to salvation?
Through the pellucid belly, long purged of earthly
nutriment,
the curvature of the knobbly spine was a dark shadow.

. . . .

A troop of doctors storms in.
At sight of the human caricature, livid on its paliasse,
they double up with paroxysms of laughter.
'He is like a splinter of ice' says one.

'Hot him up with a flask of vodka' suggests another.
'Purge him' says a third. 'Nothing to purge' growls a fourth.
A more carefully groomed figure emerges from the touzled
    group of medicos.

He pontificates thus:
'Really gentlemen, you should make use of our most
recent break-through in the clinical control of the
disorder you are engaged with, the new Bread Cure.
It was discovered in the course of an experiment,
A pretty, very pretty experiment indeed, as are all
truly scientific developments. It operates through
the simultaneous exertion of two principles,
the essence of the rye germ when transmogrificated by
the warmth of the oven will percolate through the pores
cutaneous envelope of the subject to which it is applied,
provided care has been taken to render sufficiently pliable
to admit the intrusion of the extraneous ideaform.'

The doctors do not care to engage in an argument
with an Official, and all agree that the new Bread Cure
is the precise treatment their suffering patient had need of.
'Loaves, hot loaves, an ovenful of loaves'!
And as the baker's loaded trolly reaches the prostrate Gogol,
they build around him a wall such as Jericho had, and as
the hot crust sears the lacerated flesh, Gogol screams,
but all cry out 'more loaves'! and so, disrupted beyond
bearing, Gogol withdraws himself, and obstinately dies.

For the eye-witness accounts of the great writer's last days I am indebted
to translations in David Magarshak's critical biography, *Gogol* (Faber
and Faber, 1957).

HUMAN RIGHTS YEAR 1974
Piers Plowman's Vision

In the jolly sunshine japing like jackanapes
Preening like parakeets, strode groups of grand people.
World-wide their fame ran, their least word fearful.
Braced in bright uniforms, thus they broached the business:
Stake and Fire had first speech, ancientest of forfeits;
Lash, Noose, Gibbet next, each a long nuisance;
Jack-boots-of-all-Times, and that newcomer Current;
Thumb-screw on the outskirts kept dreadfully squirming;
Gas and Bullet gossiped aloof, greatest of grave-fillers.
'I am out-numbered', nattered Bullet, 'now Napalm takes
    over.'
'And I', said newcomer Current, 'their new soles I tickle
Till some die raving and no names spoken.'
'Women are worst', whined Pincers, humblest of
    Professionals,
'Though I wrench their nails from the root.'
And many minor torments followed, tedious to total.

Their talk, this strange loss of authority.
'Our legitimate inroads resisted everywhere.
No voluntary levy from occupied outposts.'
Then up spoke a lawyer, trim in wig and diction.
'This defies Right and Reason and Rule of Law.
Let us appeal to the High Court for humane compensation.'
'I've friends on the bench', grinned Noose,
'They'll fix it for us.'

They teetered through that tall square, crying 'Taxi, taxi!'
Then glittered out of sight, too, for no soul succoured them.
Nor were those heroes of history ever heard of after
But soon the jolly sunshine was filled with light laughter.

ANCESTOR WORSHIP

We yearn to write Praise Songs
in the Afric mode! R is for Royal,
but when rulers grow crooked
who buys the cartographers' maps?
Who can then praise famous men
or the fathers that begat us?
Pietas wanes pitifully.
And the fretted canopies in our basilicas
over escutcheoned effigies of knights and ladies,
I will replace in our secular fanes
by images of other departed,
the despised and distorted
whilst the unctuous are rising
complacently into the incorruptible aether.

As I sat in the two bob launderette
watching the clothes swirl round
my thoughts slipped back to childhood days
when the wash flapped free in the drying-ground.

Her husband pushed home the huge baskets
crammed with heavy Edwardian stuff
four petticoats each and long bloomers
for a lady was hardly enough.

On Fridays he pushed back the linen
sweet smelling and ironed out so trim,
near half a ton weight he was pushing
and that meant the finish for him.

It was Lexden hill caused his collapse.
He was almost over the crest,
when he gave a great sigh and stumbled
and the wheels ran back over his chest.

She died in the Stanway Union.
Her son drowned in mud on the Somme.
One daughter made good in the Pictures,
but succumbed to the Demon Rum.

Now their cottage sells for ten thousand
but the grass bleaches linen no more:
and the cockchaffers zoom in the alders
but fade out as the Jaguars roar.

The machines are silent and still
in the darkened launderette
like a row of spacemen waiting
the daily round of the vet.

MEMO TO LORD SNOW C. B. E.

In my pram or bassinet
The Second Law of Thermodynamics
Tickled me like a frozen finger.

I

INCOMPATIBLE WORLDS
To Jonathan Swift

Boldest of the writing tribe,
master of the killing gibe,
here is work that none but you,
craftsmanlike could carry through.
When you last observed our earth
statesmen shuddered at your mirth:
you'd admit our modern themes
tax your satire's wildest dreams;
Lilliputians and Yahoos
are familiar as our shoes—
symbolise, we now confess,
Probity and Cleanliness;
grave Projectors here invent
poverty, and flesh torment;
whilst Laputan justice rules,
bombing fractious slums and schools.

You preferred the tone satiric,
used but seldom panegyric;
these times offer equal scope
for our loathing and our hope.
Now each harsh day's history craves
praise for men, and scorn for knaves,
since the same foul pigmy crew
pullulates around us, too;
crushing under bully heels
all that finely thinks or feels,
and the divergent spirit clamps
in rigid cells or sombre camps.

These would not intimidate
you who dared a savage fate,
faced a strong and ruthless foe
for a hope you could not know,
but with darkness at your back
dealt the Great a mighty crack,
battling like a classic hero
smooth-tongued tyrants vile as Nero.

Yet the bloodborn future shines
through the fury of your lines,
and its steely walls are reared
over jungle swamps you cleared.
Your negation now turns fact,
men grow noble as they act,
and the justice you invoke
men are shaping stroke by stroke,
where only energy is wealth,
and amity abundant health.

I could find no image of our totem-beasts,
ursine or feline, that weren't old familiars.
Bruin this dead o' the year snores lapped in leaves;
Grimalkin's harsh crescendo rends the frost;
but Tib domestic purrs for milk not blood;
their supernatural function's in abeyance;
fresh agents crowd in trampling ambuscade,
for the Child-god soon transcends their ancient reign.

Suddenly, through the maze of hollied trash
Gericault's *Horse* leaps to the waiting eye;
a bolt of energy transfiguring time.

That March the cottage was alive with wings.
They yearned for the garden, fluttered on the panes.
'Cannot you see there are no leaves yet,
    and rime whitens the twigs?
Stay in here where the convector heater
makes mimic Eden as the walls' bogus blooms
shed velvety petals down till ankle high.
Let your tawny images float in her deep eyes
till we've forgotten autumnal storms must rage.
Only each busy heart, tapping the breast,
links us with time and travail, seasons, grief—
when your shrivelled husks shall litter dusty sills.'

TRANSLATIONS FROM ARTHUR RIMBAUD

NOTE

These renderings of some of Rimbaud's poems were made in 1923 and 1924. A number of them were published in my biographical study, *Rimbaud: the Boy and the Poet* (Heinemann, 1924). A few revisions have since been made. It seems that my choice fell on some of those which reflect most sharply the adolescent Messianism conspicuous in his genius.

E. R.

THE DRUNKEN BOAT

As I made way along the sluggish Rivers
I sensed the haulers guided me no longer.
Squalling Redskins had seized on them for targets,
Nailing them naked to coloured stakes.

I did not give a rap for any crew,
Freighted with Flemish corn or English cottons.
When with my guides the racket died away
At the stream's whim I drifted as I'd wished.

Through the fierce clashing of the tides I dashed
Last winter, with the unresponsive mind
Of infants! and the unmoored Peninsulas
Never heard such triumphant hurley-burley.

The tempest blessed my watches on the sea;
Gay as a cork ten days I rode the waves
That some call ceaseless tossers of their prey;
Happy to miss the port-lights' stupid blink!

Delicious as crisp apple-flesh to children,
The green sea swept over my pine-wood hull,
From stains of rough red wine and caked-on vomit
Cleansed me, and carried away rudder and grappling.

And ever since, steeped in the poem Sea
Milky with the infusion of the stars,
I've devoured its glaucous depths where now and then
Gaunt flotsam, a drowned man rapt and pensive, falls;

Where, dyeing suddenly the blue, delirious
Slow rhythms under the rustling glare of day,
More vast and potent than our wine and song,
The red, raw essences of love ferment!

I know skies lightning torn, and water-spouts,
Currents and racing tides. Nightfall I know:
Dawn sweeping upwards like a race of doves.
And what man thinks he has seen, I sometimes saw.

I saw the low sun streaked with mystic horrors
Light up tall rigid figures violet-hued.
Actors they seemed in a very ancient play,
The waves that far-off clashed like slats of blinds.

Through the green night I have dreamed of dazzling snows
Rising languidly to the sea's eye.
The circulation of mysterious saps!
And that signal the blue-green phosphors chant!

I followed for whole months the maddened waves
Like rabid herds stampeding at the cliffs,
Not dreaming that the Marys' gleaming feet
Had power to muzzle Ocean's wheezy roar.

I've brushed, I tell you, incredible Floridas,
Where the flowers have eyes like those of
Man-skinned panthers, and where the rainbows
Hang under sea like reins to glaucous herds.

I have seen bubbling marshes, giant fish-pots,
Within whose reeds, entire, Leviathan rots;
Ruinous deluges from the heart of calms
And the distant waves cascading to the gulfs!

Glaciers, silver suns, and rainbow waves
And fearful strandings deep in dusky bays
Where under red-hot skies huge serpents droop
Bug-eaten, from trees twisted with black scents.

I would have wished to show those fish to children,
Those golden, singing fish leaping the blue;
Flowers of the foam have lulled me, putting out
And mysterious breezes at instants winged me.

Sometimes, a martyr wearied of poles and zones,
The sea whose soughing softened my tossing
Lifted towards me the shadow-flowers with yellow suckers
And I stayed still, like a woman on her knees.

Island, almost, I tossed on my beaches the quarrels
And the droppings and screams of the pale-eyed birds.

I sailed on, whilst through my tattered rigging
Drowned men sank down to slumber, upside down.

So I, lost boat, beneath the hair of creeks,
Or flung by tempests into birdless aether,
I whom no Monitor, or Hansa schooner
Would have fished up, a carcass drunk with water;

Free, fuming, rising out of purple mists,
Piercing the sky that ruddy as a wall
Bears the good poet's exquisite conserve,
Moss of the sunlight, snot-streaks of the blue.

Who rushed on, spangled with electric moons
Mad hulk by dark sea-elephants escorted,
While summer tempests crash with cudgel blows
The topaz sky whence red-hot funnels blaze,

Who shuddered hearing fifty leagues away
The rut of Behemoths and Maelstroms grind,
Eternal threader of the blue serene,
I regret Europe of the ancient walls!

I have seen star-archipelagos and isles
Whose madding skies lie open to the wanderer:
Do you sleep self-exiled in those endless nights,
Of countless golden birds, O future Vigour?

True, I have wept too much! Dawns rack the heart;
All moons are vile and bitter each day's sun.
Harsh love with raptest torpors bloated me.
O let my keel be shattered and the sea take me!

I long for no water of Europe but the cold
Dark puddle a sad-hearted child squats by,
Who launches out towards the scented dusk
A boat as frail as a May butterfly.

I can no longer, in your languour steeped
O waves, pick up the cotton merchants' wake
Nor now confront the pride of flags and pennants,
Nor float beneath the hulks' reproachful eyes.

VERTIGO

What does it mean to us, my heart, the pools of blood
And the embers, the thousand murders and long howls
Of fury, sobs from every sort of hell overthrowing
All order; and the north wind on the ruins still;

And all vengeance? Nothing! But still, none the less,
We will it! Industrialists, princes, senates:
Perish! Power, justice, history; Out!
It's our right. Blood! blood! the golden flame!

Everything to war, to vengeance, to terror,
My spirit! Bite deeper: Ah, pass away
Republics of this world! Of emperors,
Regiments, colonists, nations, we've had enough!

Who will stoke the whirlwinds of furious flame
But ourselves and those we believe our brothers?
Join with us, dedicated friends; this will delight us!
Never shall we do a stroke of work, o floods of flame!

Europe, Asia, America, get out of our sight!
Our avenging march has occupied all,
Cities and prairies! We shall be wiped out!
The volcanoes will explode! And the Ocean thrown back!

O my friends! Heart, it is so, they are truly brothers!
Black strangers, let us go on! Forward! Forward!
O, we perish! I feel myself shuddering, the old earth,
On me, more than ever at one with you, the earth dissolves!

It is nothing at all. I have been here all the time.

LISTEN. The story of one of my follies.

For a long time I had boasted that all possible landscapes were mine, and that I found the celebrities of modern poetry and painting ridiculous.

I liked idiotic daubs, fan-lights, stage sets, acrobats' back-cloths, sign-boards, popular prints; old-fashioned litera-ture, church Latin, erotic books with bad spelling, our grand-parents' novels, fairy-tales, the little books of childhood, old operas, silly choruses, simple cadences.

I dreamed crusades, voyages of discovery of which there are no accounts, republics without histories, the crushing of reli-gious wars, revolutions in customs, migrations of races and continents: I believed in all kinds of magic.

I invented the colours of the vowels!—A black, E white, I red, O blue, U green. I ruled the position and the movement of each consonant and I flattered myself that with instinctive rhythms I had invented a poetic language accessible one day or another to all the senses. I reserved the translation.

It was at first a study. I described silences, nights, I noted the inexpressible. I set down dizzy effects.

*   *   *   *   *

Far from the birds, the herds, the villagers,
What did I drink, kneeling in this heather,
Surrounded with the tender hazel-bushes,
In a mist of afternoon sultry and green?

What could I have drunk in this young Oise,
—Elms without voice, grass without flowers, sky overcast:—
Drunk from these yellow gourds far from my cherished
Hut? Some golden liquor which makes you sweat.

I made a dubious sign for an inn.
—A storm came to chase the blue. At dusk
The water of the woods sank in the virgin sand,
The wind of God flung icicles on the pools;

Weeping, I saw gold,—and could not drink.

*   *   *   *   *

At four in the morning, in summer,
The sleep of love endures.
Among the foliage the scents
  Of the festive eve disperse.

Down there in their vast workshop,
  In the sun of the Hesperides,
Already bustle, in shirt-sleeves,
  The Carpenters.

Quiet in their mossy Deserts
They prepare the precious panels
    Where the town
  Will paint imagined skies.

O, for these Workmen, charming
  Subjects of a king of Babylon,
Venus! leave a moment the Lovers
  Whose soul is garlanded.

  O Queen of Shepherds,
Bring to the labourers their *eau-de-vie*,
That their powers may be in repose
Awaiting the bathe in the sea at noon.

     *   *   *   *   *

The old-fashioned sorts of poetry played a considerable part in my word-alchemy.
I accustomed myself to simple hallucination: I saw quite freely a mosque in place of a factory, a school of drums formed by the angels; coaches on the roads of the sky; a drawing-room at the bottom of a lake; monsters; mysteries; the title of a musical-comedy raised up horrors in front of me.
Then I expressed the sophistries of my magic by means of the hallucination of words!
I finished by finding the disorder of my spirit sacred. I was inert, the prey of a slow fever. I envied the happiness of animals,—caterpillars, which represent the innocence of limbo; moles, the slumber of virginity. My nature became soured. I said farewell to the world in a sort of ballad:

Song of the Highest Tower

May they come, may they come,
The days which enchant us.

I have been so long resigned
That I forget it all.
Fears and sufferings
To the skies are gone,
And the unclean thirst
Darkens my veins.

May they come, may they come,
The days which enchant us.

Like the meadows
Left to ruin,
Spreading and overgrown
With incense and weeds,
In the angry humming
Of filthy flies.

May they come, may they come
The days which enchant us.

I loved waste lands, scorched-up orchards, sun-bleached shops,
tepid drinks. I dragged myself into stinking alleys and with
closed eyes I offered myself to the sun, god of fire.
'General, if there be still an old cannon on your ruined ram-
parts bombard us with lumps of parched earth. At the plate-
glass of the splendid stores! into drawing-rooms! Make the
city eat its dust. Rust the rain-spouts. Fill up the boudoirs
with a scalding powder of rubies. . . .'
Oh the little fly drunk from the inn urinal, in love with the
borage and that a ray dissolves!

Hunger

If I had any taste, it is hardly
For more than earth and stones.
I always breakfast on air,
Rock, cinders, and iron.

Round, my hungers. Crop, hungers,
   The field of sounds.
Suck the sweet venom
   Of convolvulus.

Eat the stones someone breaks,
The old stones of churches;
Boulders of ancient floods,
Loaves strewn in grey valleys.

    *   *   *   *

The wolf cries under the leaves
Spitting out the gay feathers
Of his meal of poultry:
Like him I consume myself.

Green stuffs and fruits
Await but the gathering,
But the hedge spider
Eats only violets.

May I sleep! May I boil
On the altars of Solomon.
The broth flows over the rust
And mingles with Kedron.

At last, oh happiness, oh certitude, I stripped from the sky
the azure, which is blackness, and I lived, a golden spark of
the radiance *nature*. Out of joy I chose a style as droll and far-
fetched as possible.

I have recovered it.
What? Eternity.
It is the sea merged
With the sun.

My eternal soul
Observe your vow
In spite of night alone
And the fiery day.

Then you free yourself
From human sanctions,
From common joys!
You soar thus. . . .

Never a hope,
Not a petition,
Skill and patience,
Torment is certain.

No tomorrows,
Satin embers,
Your ardour
Is your duty.

I have recovered it.
—What? Eternity.
It is the sea merged
With the sun.

I became an opera of fables: I saw that all creatures are destined to a certain contentment: action is not life, but a way of dissipating a certain power, an enervation. Morality is a weakness of the intellect.

It seemed to me that to each creature several other lives belonged. This gentleman does not know what he is doing: he is an angel. This family is a litter of dogs. With several men I have conversed aloud with a moment of one of their other lives. So, I have been in love with a pig. None of the sophistries of madness,—the madness that is shut up,—has been neglected by me: I could recite them all, I hold the system.

My health was threatened. Terror came. I fell into slumbers of many days and, risen, continued the saddest dreams. I was ripe for death, and by a road of dangers my weakness drew me to the frontiers of the world and of Chimmeria, the country of shadows and of whirlwinds.

I had to travel, to scatter the spells gathered in my head. On the sea, which I loved as though it should cleanse me of a stain, I saw the cross of salvation rise. I have been damned by the rainbow. Happiness was my destiny, my regret, my worm: my life should be always too vast to be devoted to strength and beauty.

Happiness! Her tooth, deathly sweet, warned me at cock-crow,—*ad matutinum*, at the *Christus venit*,—in the most sombre towns:

O seasons, O castles!
What soul is faultless?

I have made the magic study
Of happiness, that none evades.

Hail to it, each time
That the Gallic cock crows.

Ah! I shall have no more care:
It has taken charge of my life.

This charm has seized body and soul
And dispelled their struggles.
            O seasons, O castles!

The hour of its flight, alas!
Will be the hour of death.
            O seasons, O castles!

That is over. I know now how to acknowledge beauty.

As soon as the idea of the Flood had subsided, a hare stopped among the sainfoins and the swaying harebells, and said his prayer to the rainbow, through the spider's web.

Oh! the precious stones which hid themselves,—the flowers which looked out already.

In the dirty High Street, stalls were put up, and the barges were drawn towards the sea shelved high above as in engravings.

Blood flowed, at Bluebeard's,—in the slaughter-houses, in the circuses, where God's seal paled the windows. Blood and milk flowed.

The beavers built. The glasses of coffee steamed in the estaminets. In the great house with panes still streaming, children in mourning gazed at marvellous pictures. A door slammed; and, in the village square, the child turned his arms, followed by the wind-vanes and weathercocks all round, under the sparkling shower.

Madame *** set up a piano in the Alps. The Mass and the First Communions were celebrated at the hundred thousand altars of the cathedral.

The caravans started out. And the Hôtel Splendide was built in the chaotic, icy night of the Pole.

Since then, the Moon hears the jackals whining in the wildernesses of thyme,—and the wooden-shoed pastorals grumbling in the orchard. Then, in the violet budding forest, Eucharis told me that it was spring.

Rise, pools;—foam, flow over the bridge and pass beyond the wood;—black sheets and organs, lightnings and thunder, rise and flow;—waters and sorrows, rise and bring back the Floods. For since they have been dispersed,—oh, the precious stones hiding themselves, and the open flowers!—it is wearisome! And the Queen, the Witch who lights her embers in the earthen pot, wants never to tell us that which she knows, and of which we are ignorant.

ANTIQUE

Gracious son of Pan! Around your brows garlanded with flowerlets and with bays, your eyes, those precious globes, revolve. Stained with russet lees, your cheeks sag. Your tusks glisten. Your chest is like a cithar, tinklings pass along your golden arms. Your heart beats in that belly where sleeps the double sex. Roam you, at night, moving softly that thigh, that second thigh and that left leg.

BEING BEAUTEOUS

Against the snow, a Creature tall and beautiful. Hissings of death and dull vibrations of music make this adored body rise, swell, and tremble like a ghost; black and scarlet wounds break out in the superb flesh. The proper colours of life deepen, dance, and break loose around the vision as it forms. And the shudders rise and rumble, and the frenzied savour of these effects absorbing the deathly rattlings and raucous tones that the world, far behind us, darts at our mother of beauty, she recoils, she draws herself up. Oh! our bones are clad with an amorous new body.

O the ashen face, the horse-hair shield, the crystal arms! the cannon on which I must fling myself across the medley of trees and the limpid breeze.

LIVES

I.
O the vast avenues of the holy land, the terraces of the temple!
What has become of the Brahmin who explained the Proverbs
to me? From down here I still see even the old women of
that time! I remember hours of moonlight and of sunlight
along the rivers, my companion's hand on my shoulder, and
our caresses standing in the scorching plains.—A flight of scar-
let pigeons thunders round my thought.—Exiled here, I have
a stage on which to play the dramatic masterpieces of every
literature. I would point out to you unheard-of riches. I follow
the history of treasures that you found. I see what is to come!
My wisdom is as much disdained as chaos. What is my Nothing
beside the stupor which awaits you?

II
I am an inventor very differently deserving from all those
who have preceded me; a musician even, who has found
something like the key of love. At present, the lord of a barren
countryside with a dusky sky, I attempt to rouse myself with
the memory of my mendicant childhood, of the apprenticeship
or the arrival in sabots, of the polemics, of five or six widow-
ings, and of a few orgies where my steady head preserved me
from rising to the pitch of my comrades. I do not regret my
old part of divine gaiety: the sober air of this harsh land
nourishes most actively my atrocious scepticism. But as this
scepticism cannot henceforward be put into practice, and
besides, I am involved in a new trouble,—I expect to become
a very wretched idiot.

III.
In a hay-loft where I was shut up at twelve years old, I ex-
perienced the world, I illustrated the human comedy. In a
store-room I learnt history. At some night festival in a nor-
thern city, I met all the women of the old masters. In an
ancient passage in Paris they taught me the classic sciences. In
a magnificent dwelling, circled by the entire East, I accom-
plished my vast work and passed my illustrious retirement. I
have brewed my blood. My task is sent back to me. One must
not even dream any more of that. I am really from beyond
the tomb and no payments in advance.

DEPARTURE

Enough seen. The vision has been met in every clime.
Enough had. Murmurs of towns, at evening, and in the sun, and always.
Enough known. The summits of life.—O Murmurs and Visions!
Departure in new sympathy amid new sounds!

O my *Good*! O my *Beauty*! Excruciating fanfare where I falter not at all! Magical torture-horse! Hurrah for the never-heard-of Work and for the wonderful Body, for the first time! It began amid the laughter of children and will end with it. This poison will linger in all our veins even when, the fanfare fading, we shall be reduced to the old disharmony. O now, we so worthy of these torments! let us fervidly gather up this more-than-human promise which has been made to our created body and soul: this promise, this madness! Elegance, knowledge, violence! It has been promised us that the tree of good and of evil shall be buried in darkness, that the tyrannical proprieties shall be expelled in order that we may bring in our most pure love. It began with some revulsions and it ends—since we cannot here and now seize upon this eternity—it ends with a stampede of perfumes.

Children's laughter, slaves' discreetness, virgins' aloofness, the horror of the faces and things of this place, be sacred by the memory of this vigil! It began with all clownishness, behold, it ends with angels of flame and ice.

Brief drunken vigil, be sacred! were it only for the masque with which you have gratified us. We affirm you, Method! We do not forget that yesterday you have glorified each of our ages. We have faith in the poison. We know how to give our entire life each day.

This is the age of the ASSASSINS!

148

LABOURERS

O that sultry February morning! The unseasonable south wind brought back memories of our ridiculous beggary, our youthful misery.

Henrika had on a cotton skirt in brown and white check, which must have been worn last century, a poke-bonnet and a silk scarf. It was more miserable than mourning. We took a walk in the suburbs. The sky was overcast and that south wind roused all the vile smells of the ravaged gardens and dried-up fields.

That could not have wearied my sweetheart to the same degree as myself. In a puddle left by a flood of the previous month she pointed out to me some tiny fish.

The town with its smoke and its noise of crafts followed us a long way into the fields, O the other world, the land blessed by heaven, and its shady places! The south wind reminded me of the miserable events of my childhood, my despairs in summer, the horrible amount of power and knowledge fate has always put out of my reach. No! we will not spend the summer in this miserly country where we shall never be anything but affianced orphans. I want this hardy arm to stop lugging round cherished images.

MYSTIC

On the slope of the embankment, angels turn in their woollen dresses, in the steel and emerald herbage.

Fields of flames leap up to the top of the mount. To the left, the soil of the crest is trampled by all the homicides and all the battles, and all the disastrous noises run their curve. Behind the crest on the right, the line of dawns, of progress.

And, whilst the strip, at the top of the picture, is formed of the twisting and leaping murmur of sea-shells and of human nights,

The flowered sweetness of the stars, and of the sky, and all the rest, comes down opposite the slope, like a pannier, in front of us, and makes the abyss beneath a flowering blue.

I have clasped the summer dawn.

Nothing stirred yet on the palace fronts. The water was dead. The legions of shadows had not left the forest road. And I walked, breathing out warm, swift clouds; and precious stones looked out and wings rose without sound.

The first adventure was, in the path already filled with cool, pale flashes, a flower which told me its name.

I laughed at the pale waterfall as it tangled its hair among the pine-trees: at the silvered summit I recognised the goddess.

Then I raised, one by one, the veils. In the lane, with a shaking of arms. On the plain, where I warned the cockerel of her presence. In the city she fled among the steeples and the domes; and, running like a beggar along the marble wharves, I chased her.

At the top of the road, near a grove of laurel, I gathered her within her heaped-up veils and I felt the touch of her vast body. The dawn and the child fell together in the depths of the wood.

Wakening, it was noon.

It is possible that She might pardon me my ambitions continually crushed,—that a successful end makes up for ages of poverty,—that a day of success dulls us to the shame of our fatal ineptitude?

(O palms! diamond!—Love, strength!—higher than all joys and glories!—in every way,—everywhere, demon, god,—youth of this very creature: me!)

That the miracles of scientific magic and the progress of social fraternity should be cherished as successive restitutions of the primitive freedom?. . .

But the Vampire who makes us obedient, orders us to amuse ourselves with what she leaves us, or that otherwise we be more ridiculous.

Wallow in wounds, in the wearisome breeze and the sea: in torments, in the silence of murderous breeze and waters: in tortures which mock, in their hideously swelling silence.

SURPLUS STOCK

For sale that which the Jews have not sold, which neither nobility nor crime has relished, of which unholy love and the infernal honesty of the masses are ignorant; which neither the age nor science can perceive: Reunited Voices; the fraternal awakening of all choral and orchestral energies and their instantaneous application! The unique opportunity to liberate our senses!

For sale Bodies without price, beyond any race, class, sex, descent! Riches gushing out at each step! Sale of diamonds without control!

For sale anarchy for the masses; irrepressible satisfaction for superior amateurs; atrocious death for the faithful and lovers!

For sale habitations and migrations, sports, fairylands and perfect comforts, and the noise, the bustle, and the future they make!

For sale unprecedented applications of the calculus and leaps of harmony. Lucky finds and terms never suspected,—immediate possession. Wild and infinite leaps towards invisible splendours, insensible delights,—and for each vice its maddening secrets—and for the crowd its frightful gaiety.

For sale bodies, voices, immense unquestionable opulence, that which will never be sold. The sellers are not at the end of their stock! The travellers need not hand in their deposits so soon.